"David Lee is an exceptionally talented coach of effective communication strategies. The book is a comprehensive road map for delivering presentations with maximum impact."

Girma Wolde-Michael
Director and Senior Patent Counsel
Medtronic, Inc.

"Readers will find many helpful tips, whether they are very experienced or are giving their first speech. I will keep this book in my office as a ready reference for presentations."

Cory Nelson
VP Manufacturing Excellence
Dresser Flow Control
Dresser Inc.

"This book will be an excellent addition to management toolkits. Just like the Speaking With Impact classes, it will give the leaders in our company the confidence and know-how to present effectively. I especially like the conversational tone of the book. It makes for an easy read."

Dorothy Jeffress
Store Management Development
Corporate Human Resources
Toys "R" Us Inc.

"The tools and tips can be immediately applied to any presentation situation. It is a must-read for anyone wanting to enhance their presentation effectiveness."

Mary Poppen, M.A.
Senior HR Project Specialist,
Selection and Talent Management
Lawson Software

"I have been giving public presentations for over 25 years, and actually thought I was quite good. A working knowledge of this book would have made me a much better public speaker."

Dan Wickman, CFP
American Express Financial Advisors

By David G. Lee and Kristie J. Nelson-Neuhaus

>PRESENTATIONS
HOW TO CALM DOWN
THINK CLEARLY AND
CAPTIVATE YOUR AUDIENCE

PDI Ninth House
GLOBAL LEADERSHIP SOLUTIONS

Published by Personnel Decisions International Corporation, d.b.a. PDI Ninth House

www.pdininthhouse.com

Design: HartungKemp

Copyediting: Lynn Marasco

Indexing: Terry Casey

Typesetting and Production: Deborah Wischow

Publicity: Tami Grewenow and JoAnn Grimes

Library of Congress Cataloging-in-Publication Data

Lee, David G.

  Presentations : how to calm down, think clearly, and captivate your audience / by David G. Lee and Kristie J. Nelson-Neuhaus.

    p. cm.

Includes bibliographical references and index.

  ISBN 0-938529-23-4 (alk. paper)

  1. Business presentations. I. Nelson-Neuhaus, Kristie. II. Title.

  HF5718.22 .L425 2002

  808.5'1--dc21

                                                    2002153338

Printing Number

10 9 8 7 6 5 4 3 2

CONTENTS

ACKNOWLEDGMENTS

We would like to thank the many clients we have worked with over the years, who continually help us learn what it takes to be effective presenters. We are especially grateful to those who read drafts of the book, and provided their comments and encouragement.

We would like to thank Personnel Decisions International for providing the time, support, and funding for this project. We especially appreciate the vision and leadership of Susan Gebelein, whose sponsorship made the book possible.

> ___ FROM DAVID LEE

I wish to extend a special acknowledgment to the academic institutions where I studied and taught, which gave me a strong base for my professional work. They include Whitworth College, the University of Minnesota, Simpson College, San Francisco State University, Bethel College, and the University of St. Thomas. The most influential person in my career, Dr. Mark W. Lee, Sr. (my father), contributed enormously as my debate coach and professor of Speech-Communication at Whitworth College, and later as collaborator and encourager in my professional endeavors.

I must include a special word of thanks to my co-author, Kristie Nelson-Neuhaus. We have worked together in training and writing projects for several years. Without her skills and tenacity, we would not have completed this project.

> ___ FROM KRISTIE NELSON-NEUHAUS

I would like to thank David Lee, my colleagues at PDI, and my husband Paul. I would also like to thank my daughters, Alma and Miranda, who were very patient with their "mommy who designs with words."

INTRODUCTION

Whether you realize it or not, you probably give presentations every day. At work you might give a report at a meeting or train coworkers on a new procedure. At home you might tell family members about your day and describe in vivid detail what happened. With friends, you might reenact a conversation from work or show them something new in your house. "Wait a minute," you might be saying. "The first examples make sense because they're at work. But the other examples just sound like conversations."

Exactly! Presentations are interactive, just like conversations. Although it may seem lopsided toward the presenter doing all the work (especially if you are the presenter), the audience plays its part by paying attention, listening, laughing at humorous lines, asking questions, nodding their heads, and focusing on the presenter.

Of course, we all know there is more to it than that. Otherwise people would have no more (or less) anxiety about a presentation than they do about other conversations.

The mere thought of giving presentations makes many people queasy. Some people will do anything to avoid it, regardless of the consequences. Rather than speak in front of a group, they say, they would walk barefoot through the snow, barefoot over hot coals, barefoot over broken glass . . . you get the picture.

We believe our book will help you find the right "shoes" to help you get over your presentation fears. We will give you basic information, plus tools and tips for expanding your presentation skills.

Inside, you will find ideas on how to:

> increase your comfort in speaking to groups of all sizes.

> manage your fear instead of letting it manage you.

> connect with the audience and feel like they're for you, not against you.

> be personable and professional.

> recognize and enhance your natural style.

> make a point without saying a word.

> think on your feet.

> minimize annoying behaviors and gestures.

> improve your vocal modulation.

> pinpoint your key messages and communicate them unambiguously.

> choose compelling material that rivets your audience.

> sequence content in a strategic way.

> tailor content to an audience.

> curb a tendency to ramble and go on tangents.

Creating a presentation is a step-by-step process. We're going to take the mystery out of that process and help you turn your ideas into vibrant, multidimensional presentations.

Whether you are new to presenting, need a refresher, or are an experienced presenter looking for new approaches and ideas, this book is for you. We will inform, challenge, reassure, inspire, and encourage you.

CHAPTER 1 —— DEFINING YOUR PURPOSE

Presentations are one of the oldest forms of communication. Ancient storytellers used words, actions, and props to tell stories that riveted their listeners, expanded their imaginations, and helped them make sense of their world. Many things have changed since then, but we still tell stories. We still want to know the "real story."

Presentations are stories. Through them, people learn something they didn't know before and think about familiar topics in a new way. Presenters are storytellers. They assemble and shape information, finding precise details to convey their messages and engage their listeners. Depending on skill and information, the result can be fascinating, flat, or somewhere in between.

One of the most important steps in preparing your presentation is deciding what story you're going to tell. What do you want people to know?

> ___ SHAPING YOUR STORY

To plan your presentation, start from the center of our grid and work your way out.

1. Determine your **purpose** for the presentation.

2. Form **key messages** that will tell your story, and provide the rationale to achieve your purpose.

3. Choose **supporting material** that illuminates the key messages and supports your purpose.

4. Position your content through **strategy and style**.

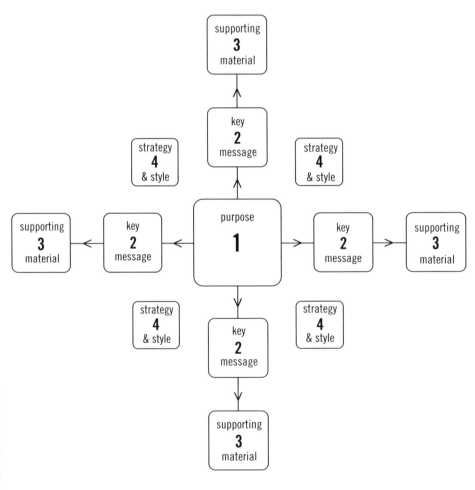

> ____ STARTING THE PROCESS

How do you typically prepare a presentation? If you are like many people, you sit down and put everything you know about a subject onto PowerPoint slides. You add lots of bullet points so you don't have to bring notes. Then you fire up the computer, dim the lights, and click and talk. Even though this may meet your colleagues' expectations, you could be wasting an opportunity to deliver a more memorable message.

Before you start gathering material or creating slides, think about your purpose. What do you want to achieve with this presentation? What can you say to this particular audience to help you achieve your purpose?

A presentation is an opportunity to assert your point of view. Even if you're giving a routine presentation, you should have an objective. This might sound too calculated, especially if you're just giving a weekly update at a team meeting. But think about it for a moment. Do you have a reason to speak, or are you just taking up airtime? If you don't have an objective, you probably should not give a presentation!

Here are some reasons to give a presentation:

> Share new information on an issue or topic.

> Advocate an idea.

> Recommend an action.

> Persuade people to try a new process.

> Update team members on progress.

> Gain approval for funding.

> Sell a product or service.

> Stimulate interest or concern.

> Inspire or initiate action.

> Evaluate, interpret, or clarify an initiative.

> Set the stage for further action.

> Explore ideas and possibilities.

> Encourage and motivate people.

To define your purpose, identify your topic in a word or phrase. Then write a sentence that states exactly what you want to accomplish by giving the presentation.

For example:

topic (word or phrase)	purpose (sentence)
Sales prospect tracking	I want to convince the sales staff to consistently use the online version of the prospect status sheet.
Company-wide quality initiative	I want to solicit one volunteer from each area for quality and productivity training.
School crowding	I want to persuade people to vote yes on a levy for building a new school.

Sometimes people make it too complicated. They come up with a grand-sounding purpose, filled with multisyllabic jargon. If you suspect that you do this, try an experiment. Tell a friend that you're giving a presentation, and then recite your purpose sentence. If you get a blank look, your purpose is unclear. Keep simplifying your purpose until it would make sense to a tenth-grader. Now your purpose is clear.

Stating your purpose in a simple way doesn't mean that you have a simple purpose. It means that you have better odds of conveying your message to your audience.

> ____ ANALYZING THE NEEDS, AUDIENCE, AND SITUATION

Now that you know your purpose, shift your focus to the context for the presentation. Take a few moments to do a Needs/Audience/Situation Analysis (NASA).

Completing a NASA will help you understand the situation so you can appropriately shape your presentation. For example, if you analyze the audience, you will understand people's familiarity with the subject and their interest level. You will also be a better judge of how much detail they need, whether they will understand your terminology, and how much context to provide in your background remarks. You can choose a structure that will help them understand the material, determine whether humor will be appropriate, and anticipate which type of visual aids they prefer.

The following questions will help you create a NASA for your presentation. These are sample questions; no doubt you will think of many more as you go along.

Needs or Opportunity

> Why are you giving the presentation? At this time? To this group of people?

> What do you need to accomplish?

> What do you want people to remember?

> If you were invited, why did they choose you?

> Is this an opportunity to communicate with people you wouldn't otherwise reach?

> How is the issue or topic important, relevant, timely, or significant to the listeners?

> How can you capitalize on their interests and expectations to reach your objective?

> Can you achieve your objective by giving a presentation, or would it be more effective to send a written document or host a discussion?

Audience

> How many people will be in the audience?

> What is the age mix of the audience?

> Do audience members have similar or dissimilar backgrounds and experience?

> Are all the people from the same company or the same department?

> What do people already know about the subject or issue?

> What do they expect to hear?

> How do people perceive your role and expertise in this situation?

  – Do they perceive you as a subject matter expert who is informing them?

  – Do they view you as a salesperson trying to convince them?

  – Do they feel overburdened by an ambitious schedule or agenda and see you as an irritating intruder on their time?

> What is your opinion of members of the audience?

> Do you agree with their assessment of the situation?

> How much interaction with the audience do you want or need?

> Will key decision makers or people who can influence decisions be in the audience?

> Do people expect (or prefer) a low-tech or a high-tech presentation?

> What kinds of presentation aids is this audience used to seeing?

Situation

> Is the occasion formal or informal?

> Where will you be presenting?

> How large is the room?

> What time of day will you be speaking?

> How much time do you have for your presentation?

> Will you sit, stand, or walk around during the presentation?

> Will you need a microphone?

> What comes right before and after your presentation?

> Are you the only presenter, or will there be several?

> Does your information contradict that of any other presenters?

> Do you want to use presentation aids?

> What equipment and resources are available for presentation aids?

> Do you need professional-quality presentation aids?

> What is your budget for presentation aids?

> Do you need to show multiple images at one time?

> ___ SAMPLE NASA

> Determine the purpose
for your presentation.

> Write down your
purpose in a clear,
concise statement.

> Decide what story
you're going to tell.
This is your opportunity
to assert your point of
view on an issue.

> Complete a NASA to
understand the needs
for the presentation,
the situation, and the
audience.

> Tailor your presenta-
tion to the audience's
experiences, familiar-
ity with the topic, and
expectations.

Needs

I've been asked to present my unit's goals for next year. I'm supposed to explain each goal, discuss why we set it, and show how it is aligned with other units' goals and with the organization's strategic priorities. The stakes are high, since our unit did not do well last year. People want to know how my goals are going to improve the bottom line. I am new to the organization and need to make a good impression and show my expertise.

Audience

My boss (general manager for our division), my peers (who will be presenting their units' goals at the same meeting), the CFO, COO, and CEO. Total of ten people at the meeting, but only six presenters. "Integration" and "seamless service" are the buzzwords this year, and I have to show how my unit is going to work with other groups to achieve them. I have been told that the CEO does not suffer fools gladly, so I have to be ready to answer tough, targeted questions.

Situation

We are meeting in the boardroom, which has an overhead projector, flip charts, a whiteboard, and a projector for a laptop computer. People will be seated around a table, and will go to the head of the table while they present. The meeting is from 2:00 to 4:00 P.M. Each presenter will have 20 minutes, which will include time for questions. We have been told not to go over our time limit, since the CEO has to leave for a flight by 4:10. Unfortunately, two of my peers have a tendency to go over their time limit, and the person facilitating this meeting lets them. I need to make sure that I go first or second, so I don't get shortchanged on time.

CHAPTER 2 —— CORE CONTENT

Presentations are aural structures. Like all structures, they need a foundation. This foundation has to be solid and well made, so it can carry the weight of all the elements of the presentation.

The foundation of your presentation is composed of key messages, or core content. They define your topic. Because of them, your presentation has structure, meaning, and focus. Because of them, the audience knows what your story is about and understands the main points of the plot.

> —— CRAFTING KEY MESSAGES

Building the foundation for your presentation takes time. You may find that it is a process in which key messages determine the type of information you're looking for, and the information you find shapes your key messages. Sometimes you need to write down several thoughts and slowly distill them. At other times, you may know the general messages immediately but need to refine them as you work on the rest of the presentation.

When you formulate key messages, don't get stalled by trying to make them perfect the first time you write them. Just write down your thoughts. Then, as you refine them, use these guidelines.

> Write a declarative sentence, not just a phrase.

> Include only one idea in each sentence.

> Make each key message believable.

> State the message in a positive way (if you can).

> Use language that is appropriate to you, to the subject, and to the listeners.

> Avoid emotional, argumentative, or "loaded" language.

> Choose precise, apt words that have impact.

> Use words that appeal to the senses (touch, see, hear).

> Use active rather than passive verbs.

> Delete extra words.

> Create vivid descriptions.

> Limit use of abbreviations, acronyms, and technical jargon.

> Delete expressions like "maybe," "perhaps," "probably," "I think," and "sort of."

Here is an example from a presentation on the qualities of admired leaders. Note that the key messages have a similar rhythm, which makes it easier for the audience to recognize and remember them.

> Effective leaders demonstrate Vision.

> Effective leaders demonstrate Integrity.

> Effective leaders demonstrate Patience.

> Effective leaders demonstrate Persistence.

> Effective leaders demonstrate Passion.

People wonder how many key messages they should put into their presentations. A general guideline is three to five, regardless of the length of the presentation. Audiences only remember up to five messages at one time.

Even if you have several hours, resist the temptation to add more messages. Instead, use the extra time to develop your key messages more thoroughly by including more supporting material, or hold a discussion with the audience.

> ___ ORGANIZING YOUR MATERIAL

If you like to organize information, you will have a great time working on your presentation. First, you can organize the information on the broadest level by deciding what to put in the introduction, core content, and conclusion. Then you can move on to the sequence of your key messages. Next you can develop the content within each key message.

An organizing structure helps you understand the flow of your presentation. The structure reveals whether your key messages relate well to each other, and whether you have all the supporting material you need and want.

Following are several common structures for presentations.

Acronym

Create an acronym from the beginning letter of each key message or primary word within your key messages. Use an acronym only if it readily fits your key messages. Don't force it to fit.

Audience Expectations

Begin with the points that the audience wants and expects to hear. For example, if your organization is restructuring, employees will want to know if they still have jobs, or if their jobs will change. If you delay in discussing their most pressing questions, people will feel anxious throughout your presentation and have a difficult time concentrating on your other points.

Chronological

Arrange events in the order of their occurrence. This structure works well for describing events that took place during a given period, or processes that require a sequence of steps or stages.

Classification

Group your key messages into categories. For example, your presentation may cover the categories of research and development, engineering, manufacturing, and sales.

Climax

Arrange your key messages in order of increasing importance, ending with the most compelling and convincing. For example, in reviewing recent business performance, one executive had four key messages:

1. Recent results in region A have been on target.

2. Recent results in region B have been uneven.

3. Recent results in region C have been disappointing.

4. Recent results in region D have been devastating.

Deductive and Inductive

To use a deductive structure, describe an accepted general premise and back it up with specific issues or examples. This works well when you are testing or confirming an idea by showing that each instance supports it.

To use an inductive structure, begin with specific details, find themes and patterns, and (like a detective) draw a broad conclusion. Use this approach to show how you arrived at a conclusion by taking people on your journey of discovery.

Funnel

Categorize your material by breadth of content, and begin with the broadest category. For example, a presentation on an organization's status might move from how it fares in the global arena, to the national arena, to within the industry.

Level of Complexity

Arrange your key messages from the simplest to the most complex. This works especially well with unfamiliar, difficult, or complicated ideas, since you build a foundation as you proceed.

Problem/Solution/Advantages

Present a problem, suggest a solution, and indicate the likely advantages of your solution.

Process of Elimination

Describe a problem and list several potential solutions. Then talk about each option, showing why it is insufficient or unworkable. End with the solution you support, and explain why it is the best choice.

The "Star"

When you want to tailor the same presentation for different audiences, and it is clear there is one central theme for your material, use the Star.

Discuss your central theme first, giving any necessary background or context. Then use a transition statement, such as a question, to move out to a key message on one of the "rays." After you present the supporting material, use a summary statement to move back to the center. Repeat this pattern for each key message.

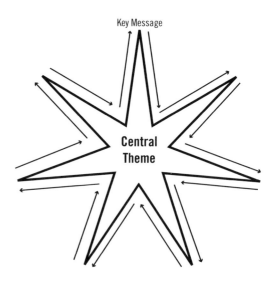

Key Message

Central Theme

When you use the Star, it's easy to tailor the same presentation for different audiences. All you have to do is choose key messages (rays) for each audience. The central theme remains the same.

Unifying Device

A unifying device is an element—a metaphor, story, theme, word, comparison, quote—that you use several times during a presentation.

For example, an executive giving a presentation to employees said: "The last 18 months have been like a raft trip on the

Colorado River. We have hit a lot of rapids, boulders in the river, and bends we didn't or couldn't see around." Later in the presentation he talked about "navigating on turbulent waters," saying that "those of us still on the raft are exhausted, yet here we go again," and referring to lessons from the "whitewater."

> ___ SUPPORTING YOUR KEY MESSAGES

Supporting material provides evidence for your key messages. As you find material to support your key messages, remember one fundamental fact: presentations are illustrative, not comprehensive. What does this mean? It means that you can't pack everything you know or discover about the topic into your presentation. Our advice: choose short, concise material that makes your point.

To get started, write down your key messages. Underneath each one, list the information you already have and the areas you would like to explore further. For example:

Key message: your department exceeded its revenue goals last year.

Information you already have: quarterly and year-end reports, list of goals.

Areas you want to explore further: compare your results to the goals (create a chart), interview people in the department for details (statistics and quotes), analyze how your accomplishments supported the larger organization.

As you search for material, apply these criteria:

> Is the material appropriate for your audience? Will they understand it?

> Is the information clearly relevant to your key message?

> Is the material sufficiently detailed to make your point?

> Do you believe the information? Can you present it with conviction?

> ___ CHOOSING SUPPORTING MATERIAL

The best presentations include a mix and variety of supporting material. Here are five types you can choose from.

Comparisons

Comparisons indicate similarities and dissimilarities between objects, events, projects, issues, and experiences. Comparisons also allow you to use something familiar to explain something unfamiliar. You use comparisons every day, when you say something "is better than," "not as good as," "similar to," or "resembles" something else.

Determine whether you should use gender-neutral and culture-neutral metaphors. For instance, music can be used as a metaphor for nearly anyone—most people have been involved in music as a student, performer, or listener.

Sample comparisons
> When you squeeze a sponge, you find out what type of liquid is inside it. When life puts pressure on you, what will you find? Compassion, respect, and sensitivity—or resentment, anger, and bitterness?

> Fire requires three necessary and sufficient conditions: a fuel, oxygen, and a source of heat. Unless you have all three conditions, you will not have a flame. A business initiative may have some of the necessary conditions, but they are not sufficient to produce the desired outcome.

Examples

Simple, concrete examples, including illustrations and anecdotes, are excellent ways to convey meaning. Audiences usually find examples easier to understand than explanations because examples are less abstract.

Look for examples that match your point in tone and complexity. To make a simple point, use a simple example. If you use a hypothetical example, make sure that it is believable and contains elements that are familiar to your listeners.

Sample examples

> There are good ideas all around you; the secret is to be alert. In the 1940s, Edwin Land took a photograph of his little daughter at the beach and she asked him, "Why can't I see the picture now, Daddy?" That innocent question sparked an idea that led him to develop the Polaroid camera.

> Sometimes simple, straightforward instructions can be confusing. One parent noticed her son had a note on his computer with a password of "MickeyMinnieGoofyPluto" and asked why it was so long. The boy explained that the instructions told him to choose a password with at least four characters.

Explanations

Explanations describe or define something: a term, a process, a program, a product. Because explanations can be abstract, be sure to combine them with a strong example or comparison to make them comprehensible.

Be aware that presenters often overuse explanations. If your presentations seem to drag or you speak in a monotone, check to see how many explanations you use. Adding more types of supporting material may be the key to making your presentations more engaging.

Sample explanations

> Adult learners tend to be self-directed, interested in personal development, and focused on skills that will help them improve their performance immediately.

> A scenario building technique allows people to think freely about the future, while providing an organizing structure for their thoughts.

Quotations

A pithy, well-chosen quote from a historical figure, a well-known personality, a client, an industry expert, or an organizational leader can add color, excitement, and credibility to your presentation. Before you use a quote, verify that you have copied it correctly. Don't rely on your memory—look it up.

Sample quotations

"We are all manufacturers. Making good, making trouble, or making excuses."
                                        —*H. V. Adolt*

"Anyone who says businessmen deal only in facts, not fiction, has never read old five-year plans."   —*Malcolm Forbes*

"Even if you're on the right track, you'll get run over if you just sit there."
                                        —*Will Rogers*

Statistics

Statistics concretely summarize quantitative information. Used well, statistics can surprise, shock, enlighten, delight, entertain, inform, or provoke an audience. Used poorly, statistics can evoke yawns and looks of disbelief.

> When you use statistics, state them in compre-hensible figures. Make them comparative whenever possible (for example, this year's results compared with last year's).

> Use statistics to support the point you're making. Don't just throw in random numbers.

Sample statistics

> Research shows that up to 93 percent of people's interpretation of attitudes is based on nonverbal communication.

> Young adults with college degrees earn over 70 percent more than those without, and those with high school diplomas earn 30 percent more than those without.

> ___ USING HUMOR

KEY POINTS TO REMEMBER

> Declare your point of view through your key messages.

> Write a concise declarative sentence—not just a phrase—for each key message.

> Use no more than three to five key messages during a presentation.

> Select an appropriate organizing structure for your key messages.

> Don't try to cover every aspect of a topic in one presentation.

> Include at least five types of supporting material in your presentation.

> Make sure supporting material is clearly relevant to your key messages.

> Adapt content to your audience's needs.

Humor grabs the audience's attention and helps people relate to you on a personal level. You can use humor to warm up a group, provide comic relief, establish a perspective in a challenging situation, or wryly illustrate a serious point. Humor doesn't consist solely of one-liners and jokes. An element of humor—a humorous quote, story, or example— can be included in any type of supporting material.

Sample humorous statistic

Richard Leider, author and guru on work/life balance and dealing with stress, introduces a statistic in the following manner: "It is estimated that up to one-third of adults suffer symptoms commonly associated with work-related stress. Look at the person sitting on your left and the person on your right. Do they both look calm? If so, that indicates who the one-in-three is: *you.* "

CHAPTER 3 ___ INTRODUCTIONS, TRANSITIONS, AND CONCLUSIONS

Giving a presentation is like guiding a tour group. When you travel with a group, you need to accommodate a wide range of needs. Low-maintenance people need little reminding, prodding, or coddling. They're content to take each day as it comes, and they enjoy most activities. Other people want details about every item on the itinerary. They want to know where you'll be taking them, how you're going to get there, and what you'll see along the way. They want reminders each morning, updates at lunch, and recaps every evening.

As you guide the audience through your presentation "journey," your introduction, transition statements, and conclusion will help you lead people through unfamiliar territory and keep them on track. The introduction will tell the group where you're going and how you're going to get there. Transitions will confirm how far you have come and remind people of what's next. The conclusion will help you review highlights of the trip and tell people what to do when they get home.

> ___ INTRODUCTIONS

Most people decide within the first 20 seconds to two minutes if they think you are worth listening to. With this kind of pressure, you can't afford to flub your introduction.

First impressions are difficult to change, so set the right tone. If you establish rapport and generate interest in your topic, people will give you a chance. If you deliver a boring, static introduction, the audience will tune out, daydream, and probably ignore most of your presentation.

Your introduction should do three things: grab the audience's attention, provide appropriate background information, and introduce your key messages. What will get people's attention? A statement that engages them and makes them think. Here are some ideas you can try:

> Make a dramatic statement. Pause momentarily after the statement to give it more impact and give the audience a chance to absorb it. For example: "Can you imagine evacuating 50,000 people from a city in a single afternoon? The mayor of Grand Forks, North Dakota, had to do it when the Red River was rising rapidly in 1997."

> Refer to a recent or well-known event. Most people in the audience will immediately conjure up their own images or impressions of the event and wonder what you're going to say next.

> Tell a personal story. Choose a story that relates to your purpose; don't just talk about yourself for the sake of talking about yourself. Audiences can tell the difference.

> Tell a humorous story or use a humorous quote. But remember that humor is a high risk/high reward element that needs to be done well.

> Describe a scenario or situation. Either outline a situation in which the audience fills in the details, or use a complete example in which you interpret the events.

> Redefine something familiar in a way that startles people. For example, "Some people will tell you that customers are always right. I'm here to tell you that customers are often wrong, and it is your job to tell them so!"

> Use a quote or a testimonial from a well-respected, authoritative source.

> Ask the audience a question. If you choose this option, be aware that you may hear answers that are completely unrelated to your topic, so be prepared to continue regardless of the response.

Providing Background Information

Why should you provide background on your subject? First, you can't assume that the audience knows why you are giving the presentation. They may have a general sense of what you're going to talk about but not understand the specific context. Second, people in the audience may have varying degrees of familiarity with your topic. Background information gives them a similar starting point. Third, this is a chance for you to position your message and clarify why it is important to the listeners.

Often people underplay or skip the background section in their introduction. Then they try to make up for it by giving detailed explanations during their key messages. This confuses the audience, since it seems like the speaker is backtracking, or explaining the same thing several times.

What should you do in the background?

> Declare your objective for the presentation.

> Define your point of view on the issue or topic.

> Briefly outline the history and context of the situation. Choose details that illuminate the situation; don't bury people with tangential information.

> Establish that you have a shared interest in making a decision or getting something accomplished.

> Indicate why the issue or topic is important to the audience.

Introducing Key Messages

Now that you have people warmed up, it's time to tell them precisely what you're going to cover during the rest of the presentation. Introducing your key messages will tell people what to expect and when they can expect it.

People tend to listen to presentations on two levels. On the surface, they listen to your words. Below the surface, they try to understand what you've said, anticipate what you're going to talk about next, and predict your conclusion. An overview gives them the big picture so they can focus on the details.

Keep in mind that people are listening to you, not reading a document. Repeating your key messages at least three times (overview, core content, and conclusion) will make it more likely that people will recognize and remember them. Some people refer to this as "tell them what you're going to talk about, talk about it, then tell them what you talked about."

> ___ TRANSITIONS

Transitions help you and your listeners stay on course throughout the presentation. They help you move smoothly from one key message to the next. Back to our traveling metaphor, transitions are like verbal signposts. They tell you where you are at the moment, where you are in relation to the entire trip, and where you're going next.

Transitions can be verbal, nonverbal, or both. To make a nonverbal transition, you can drop or raise your voice, pause, take a step, or gesture in a way that suggests the completion of one idea and the start of another. To make a verbal transition, you can use anything from a single word to several sentences. For example:

Single word: first, second, third, furthermore, next, finally.

Phrase: in the first place, on the other hand, in addition, not only . . . but also, keep in mind, another factor we must consider, a second lesson we learned, in summary, in closing.

Sentence: Next, let's discuss why the product launch was so successful.

Question: Why was the product launch so successful?

Here are four ways to make a smooth transition:

> Summarize the previous point(s).

> Forecast the next point.

> Provide both a summary and a forecast.

> Ask a question, then answer it with your next key message.

> ___ CONCLUSIONS

How many times have you breathed a sigh of relief when you heard the words "in conclusion"? And then gritted your teeth when the person proceeded to speak for another 10 minutes? You probably remember the presentation as being tedious and meandering, and promptly forgot the speaker's key messages.

Listeners like to feel a sense of completion at the end of a presentation. To give them this sense, do three things:

1. **Briefly recap your key messages.**
   When you review your key messages, use your original declarative sentences. Don't go into details on the messages; you just did that during the presentation.

2. **Emphasize one point (final emphasis).**
   Assume that individuals will remember only one thing you said. Also assume that they will probably remember best what you said last. What do you want it to be?

It might be one of your key messages, or a broader point that ties your key messages together. Always strive to send people off with an emphasis that is so clear and self-evident that they can't forget it.

3. **Tell the audience what you'd like them to do in response to your presentation (implication statement).**

    Too many presenters simply say "thank you" and flee. They squander an opportunity to unambiguously tell the audience how to respond. Take time to think about how you want people to respond to your presentation. You don't want to be caught speechless when people ask how they can help or participate.

    An implication statement puts the focus on the audience. According to one dictionary definition, to implicate is "to involve in the nature or operation of something." This is precisely what you want to do with the audience—involve them. In fact, you could think of this section of your presentation as the "involvement statement." It's where you answer the audience's "so what?" and "what's in it for me?" questions.

    What types of things should you ask for? Depending on your purpose, you might ask for approval for a plan or a budget, for involvement and support in a change initiative, for ideas and comments on a proposal, or for a vote of support.

> ___ INTRODUCING ANOTHER SPEAKER

Occasionally, you may be asked to introduce another speaker at a business or social function. You can structure your introduction by using the building blocks of a presentation. For example:

Introduction	**attention getter**
	short anecdote about the person
	background
	person's name, professional achievements, why he or she was asked to speak about the topic
	overview of key messages
	the person's topic is timely for these reasons
Core Content	**key messages**
	briefly describe the speaker's topic
Conclusion	**recap key messages**
	(skip this if the introduction lasts five minutes or less)
	final emphasis
	we eagerly anticipate hearing the person's viewpoint on the topic
	implication statement
	please welcome (person's name)

Here are some additional guidelines:

> First impressions are difficult to change, so set the right tone with your introduction.

> Give people an overview so they can relax and listen to the details.

> Use transitions to move smoothly from one key message to the next.

> Learn how to use both verbal and nonverbal transitions.

> Give listeners a sense of completion at the end of your presentation.

> Emphasize one final point.

> Take advantage of the "recency effect": people remember best what you say last.

> Don't rely on spontaneous inspiration. Write out the entire introduction, or thoroughly outline it. Limit ad-libs.

> Select material from the person's résumé. Don't simply recite the whole thing.

> Resist showering the person with praise and promising that the speech will be great. Instead, clarify why the speaker is qualified to speak about the topic.

> Avoid clichés such as "a speaker who needs no introduction" (why are you giving an introduction?).

> Don't preempt the speaker's topic. If you discuss it too thoroughly, you may incorrectly describe one of the key messages or contradict the speaker.

> Create an introduction that builds up to the point where the speaker stands and walks to the lectern.

> Don't overdo it. Too dynamic an introduction is a hard act for the speaker to follow.

CHAPTER 4 — PRESENTATION AIDS

Which do you remember longer: an image or a description? If you're like many people, you can recall an image more readily. In many countries, especially the United States, people live in a visual culture. Television monitors are everywhere: in airports, restaurants, stores, homes, vehicles, sports arenas. People instantly recognize brand images from across the world. Music videos are a must for recording artists. The Internet has streaming media. Is it any wonder that people like (and expect) a visual component in presentations?

People tend to believe what they see more than what they hear, even though they know that images can be manipulated. They want to see the pictures.

Since we live in an image-filled age, why not use presentation aids all the time? Because they can take over your presentation. Imagine the following scene. You're giving a presentation. Behind you is a large window through which the audience can see people walking past, traffic, the shadows of leaves throwing patterns across the floor, and the occasional squirrel. You gradually realize that people are looking through the window instead of at you. When someone passing by the window stops to wave, you finally pull the blinds or shut the curtain.

Now imagine that you're giving a presentation during which there is the constant hum of a projector, and words or images are constantly being flashed behind you. You're splitting your focus between managing the visuals and speaking to the audience. Sometimes you step back, and the image is superimposed on your face.

Both situations have the same effect: there is competition for the audience's attention. In the first case, outside elements are a distraction from your messages; in the second, you create your own distraction.

> ___ BENEFITS OF PRESENTATION AIDS

Presentation aids are documents, props, media, people, or other elements that you use to convey your message. They can be as simple as your notes, which aid you personally, or as complex as live video feeds from all over the world. They help you appeal to people's senses, and to crisply and economically make your point. They also help you:

> add humor

> aid retention

> encourage participation

> explain a difficult concept

> focus attention

> kindle interest

> persuade listeners

> prevent misunderstandings

> reinforce ideas

Example

Sarah told people repeatedly that sales had been going up over the past three years, but they didn't seem to understand that the growth was dramatic. So she created a graph that showed the first three years as relatively flat, then sharp spikes in each of the next three years.

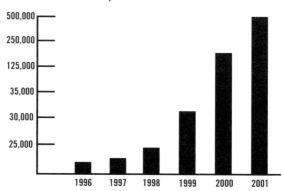

Every presentation aid should have a purpose. You should be able to explain exactly why you chose it, what you expect to accomplish by using it, and why it is a better choice than simply conveying the concept with words.

If you emphasize everything visually, in effect, you emphasize nothing.

If you can't explain the need for an aid, it's probably not necessary. This can be a painful fact for people who are used to putting everything on slides and calling it a day. They aren't accustomed to going through the selection process. They find it more efficient to use presentation notes as visuals.

Although it may be efficient, it's often less effective. People miss an opportunity to use presentation aids to their advantage. It's like having a Steinway piano and using it only to play "Chopsticks." The piano works well for this purpose, but people never get an opportunity to hear it played as it could be played. And soon they think pianos were made only for playing "Chopsticks."

When you're trying to decide whether you need a presentation aid, start with your content. Examine your key messages and supporting materials with an eye to adding visuals or audio. For example, are you:

> Using several explanations to convey a complicated issue? Show a series of visuals.

> Outlining a process? Use a flowchart.

> Describing a place? Show a photograph.

> Introducing a product? Hold up a sample.

> Showing a change? Use graphs or charts.

> Explaining a journey or itinerary? Show a map with the route marked.

> Evoking a long-gone era? Play music from the period.

> Reciting statistics? Use a bar chart, pie chart, or line graph.

CHAPTER 4 —— BENEFITS OF PRESENTATION AIDS

31

> A RANGE OF OPTIONS

Most people think of handouts, overheads, and PowerPoint slides, but the range of options is limited only by your topic and your imagination. Here are some ideas to get you started:

> animation

> art

> audio clips

> banners

> cartoons

> charts

> computer graphics

> costumes

> demonstrations

> diagrams

> dramatic sketch or skit

> drawings (done during the presentation)

> flip charts

> flowcharts

> handouts

> live audio, Internet, or television hookup

> maps

> music, live or recorded

> overheads

> people (performers)

> photographs or slides

> posters

> presentation software

> props (product samples, clothing, food, tools)

> puppets

> storyboards

> video clips

> Web sites

> whiteboards

> ___ GENERAL TIPS AND GUIDELINES

The quality of your aids signifies the quality of your presentation. People tend to believe what they see, so it is to your advantage to create aids that enhance, not undermine, your message.

> Pay attention to how text and images appear in magazines, newspapers, books, Web sites, and other media. Save examples of things you like or would like to try in your presentations.

> Create "design specs" for your presentation. Include color, layout, font, type size, and other items that need to be consistent.

> Lay out all your presentation aids in the order in which you plan to use them.

   – Check the sequence. Does it flow?

   – Are you repeating any aids? Should you?

   – All they all necessary? Remove some of them and see how it affects your presentation.

> Assess the images. Do they support, contradict, or compete with your key messages?

> Check for clutter. Do the visuals look dense and complex, or did you build in enough white space?

> Use a series of simple visuals rather than a single complex visual.

Text and Color

> Choose a font that is legible from the back of the room where you will be presenting.

> Limit the number of fonts on a single presentation aid. The most common combination is to use a sans serif font for titles or headings and a serif font for text.

> Make the text large and legible. Use at least 32-point type for titles, 24-point for subtitles, and 18-point for text.

> Follow the 1x5x5 rule: no more than five words per line, no more than five lines per slide. Do this by using key words and phrases instead of sentences.

> Avoid using ALL CAPS (it's like shouting) or all lowercase. Instead, use typical sentence structure: the first letter of the first word capitalized, and the rest of the words lowercase.

> Limit the number of colors you use. Too many colors can be difficult to read or give you eye fatigue.

> If you are representing your organization, find out if there are corporate color guidelines you need to follow.

> Be aware of the meaning of color in the culture where you are presenting. For example, white means purity in some cultures, death in others.

Proofreading Tips

> Check your accuracy. Proofread your presentation aids, then ask an expert proofreader to read your materials. Compare your versions to see what you've missed, then watch for similar mistakes in the future.

> Catch typographical errors by starting at the last word and working your way backward, one word at a time.

> Use a computer spell check only as a first sweep for general errors. It won't catch words that are spelled correctly but used incorrectly.

Create a checklist that you can use each time you proofread presentation aids. Include items such as:

> consistent use of fonts, font sizes, bold, and italic

> capital letters at the beginning of sentences

> missing, inconsistent, or incorrect punctuation at the end of sentences

> punctuation within sentences

> words that are cut off

> misplaced apostrophes

> agreement between subject and verb

> both parts of pairs: quotation marks, parentheses, brackets

> symbols for trademarks and registered trademarks

> capitalized proper nouns

Make sure the following items are correct:

> acronyms

> alphabetical sequences

> calculations

> captions and labels

> headers and footers

> numerical sequences

> page numbers

> quotations

> statistics

> tables and figures

> ⎯ USING PRESENTATION AIDS

Some presenters spend hours carefully designing and preparing their presentation aids, then simply nod at them or underplay them during the presentation. This leaves the audience wondering why they used an aid and how it was relevant to the topic.

When you use a presentation aid, follow this sequence:

1. Prepare a statement to introduce each aid to the audience. Give the audience some context for what they're seeing or hearing. This will heighten their sense of anticipation and prepare them for what's coming next.

2. Display the aid.
   - Display the aid when it relates to your point.
   - Avoid standing between the aid and your audience. Blocking the sight line irritates listeners.
   - Determine if you need to maintain eye contact with the audience while you display the aid. For example, if you're showing a video clip or there are performers,

watch the video or the performers instead of looking at the audience. If you're showing an overhead, maintain eye contact with the audience.

3. Describe the essential elements of the aid and make your point.

    –   Elaborate on the message of the aid, but don't simply repeat it. (In other words, don't read slides or overheads verbatim.)

    –   Glance at the aid when necessary, but don't address your comments to it. Look at the audience while you talk.

    –   Speak with more volume than is normally required: the listener's attention is divided between you and the aid. If you're using a projector, remember that most projectors make some noise.

4. Move smoothly into the next segment of the presentation. Keep talking as you move on to the next point. A long pause will break your momentum.

Here are some tips for using presentation aids. The aids are presented in alphabetical order.

Audio and Video

>   Watch or listen to the entire clip in advance so you won't be surprised by anything on it.

>   Cue up tapes and CDs to the starting point so they will be ready to go.

>   Test the equipment before you begin the presentation. (You'd be surprised how many people skip this step.)

>   Check the sound level to make sure everyone in the room can hear it without straining or being deafened.

Flip Charts and Whiteboards

> Recognize that writing on flip charts and whiteboards takes time. Account for this time when you plan your presentation.

> Consider preparing some or all of your flip charts in advance.

> Bring a set of markers with you. Make sure they are appropriate for the surface (don't use paper markers on a whiteboard, for example).

> Use dark-colored markers for better contrast and legibility.

> Alternate between two colors when you are writing lists.

> Write in large, legible letters.

> Learn how to draw simple images and graphs that you can quickly replicate.

> Occasionally turn toward the audience while you write, so you can maintain some eye contact.

> Use overheads or presentation slides when there are more than 40 people in the audience. People may have difficulty reading a flip chart or whiteboard from all parts of the room.

Handouts

> In general, distribute handouts after your presentation. Otherwise the audience will read your handouts instead of listen to you.

> Make an exception and provide handouts during the presentation when you want people to refer to them, or you want to read sections of the handout aloud.

> If you expect the audience to take notes, hand out a brief outline of your presentation, then provide more detailed handouts after you finish presenting.

> Build interest in your handouts by giving a preview of what people will find in them.

> Bring along extra copies of all handouts. There may be more people in the audience than you expected.

> Create a tag line that captures your key point and use it as a header on handouts.

> When you create handouts from a PowerPoint presentation:

  – Print the slides as handouts (set this up on the print screen).

  – Instead of copying every slide, copy only the most important slides so you don't inundate people with information. (You may also want to take this opportunity to assess whether you have too many slides in your presentation.)

  – Add interpretive remarks to slides, if necessary.

Notes

Audiences expect presenters to use notes. In fact, if you don't have notes and are highly competent, you may be perceived as being too smooth or slick. When you use notes, remember these tips:

> Use notes openly. Trying to cover up your notes will distract your audience. Use a lectern, if one is available. Otherwise, hold your notes at a level where you can see them easily instead of looking down at a steep angle.

> Write or print clearly. Create notes that allow you to see your key messages with a quick glance, so you can maintain eye contact with the audience. Use a dark felt pen and write in large, legible letters. Consider using five-by-eight-inch cards for your notes. Card stock is easier to handle than paper; it won't bend and flutter. These cards are also large enough to accommodate relatively large writing or printing.

> Include only the level of information you need. Notes are meant to keep you organized and prompt your memory with key words, phrases, and figures. Include only the information you need. If one word on a card is enough, then use only one word. If you need a few more details, include them as well.

> Practice with the notes. Practicing with notes will increase your confidence. When you hold notes, avoid twisting, bending, or playing with them.

> Speak, don't read. You will be more effective if you speak from notes than if you read from a manuscript. You will have a more natural, fluent delivery, and the words will reflect your style. Also, people will view you as more knowledgeable and sincere because you're speaking from your own knowledge and experience.

Overheads

> Number your overheads. This will help you put them together quickly if you drop them or they get out of order.

> Put overheads in a three-ring binder so you can flip through them easily.

> Focus the projector before you start your presentation.

> Arrange the projector and screen so all audience members can see the screen.

> Practice putting overheads on and taking them off the projector. This may seem simple, but it takes practice to put them on straight, not backwards, and not fumble with finding the next slide or putting the old one aside.

> Limit yourself to one overhead for every one or two minutes of speaking. Otherwise you'll spend too much time on the mechanics of switching overheads.

> Choose landscape rather than portrait orientation for overheads (the long side at the top and bottom instead of at the sides). This will let you use a larger font. Also, it will keep the text higher on the screen so it won't get cut off by the edges of the projector.

> If you want to call attention to a particular section of the overhead, point on the projector instead of walking to the screen.

> Instead of putting detailed data tables on an overhead, show only the key data or summarize the conclusions.

> Include a frame around overheads to give them a finished, consistent look.

People/Performers

> Meet with performers beforehand to describe the purpose of your presentation. Impress on them what you're trying to accomplish and why you're involving them.

> Rehearse with the performers.

  – Go through the entire presentation to work
    out the logistics and timing.

  – Rehearse in the space where you will give the
    presentation.

  – Rehearse in front of a group, if possible.

> Give people a time frame for how long the
  performance should last.

> Choose a signal you can use if they go over the
  allotted time.

> Watch the group or individuals perform in other
  venues to see how they react under pressure.

PowerPoint

People have strong opinions about PowerPoint. Some people
swear by it, others swear at it. We see it as a neutral tool,
albeit one that is often overused.

When you use PowerPoint, consider whether you're using it,
or it's using you. Are you changing your thoughts or your
material because it doesn't fit neatly onto slides? When you
use PowerPoint, consider these suggestions:

> Use the Master Page feature to repeat elements,
  such as a company logo, on every page.

> When you want to create suspense, use builds
  (show one bullet at a time) to create a list. Use
  the same style of build each time; otherwise, your
  audience will start paying attention to what is
  going to happen next rather than to what you
  will say next.

> Keep transitions (fading in, spiraling out) to a
  minimum.

> Create a visual pause in your presentation by inserting a solid black slide.

> Resist putting every word on your slides. Remember that slides are not presentation notes. The 1x5x5 guideline [see page 34] applies here.

> Learn how to use the features smoothly. Fumbling with technology will make you nervous and distract the audience.

> Rehearse your presentation in front of a colleague. Learn whether you are overusing any features or functions.

> If you don't want to focus on technology, ask a colleague to advance the slides and handle the equipment.

> Be ready if the equipment crashes. Either bring printed handouts of your slides or copy your slides onto standard overhead transparencies.

> Recognize that presenting in a semi-darkened room will decrease eye contact with the audience and will inhibit note taking and discussion.

Memorize a statement you can use when there are hitches with your presentation aids. Keep it lighthearted and positive.

Props

> Choose props that support your message, not detract from it.

> Check your props to make sure you have the correct ones. You don't want to make a big lead-in to a new product, only to hold up one with last year's packaging.

> Put your props where you can reach them easily.

> Practice handling props so you don't drop them, and so you aren't surprised by their weight or bulk.

> Visually or audibly
reinforce important
messages with pre-
sentation aids.

> Make sure presentation
aids do not contradict
or compete with your
key messages.

> Use presentation aids
to portray something
that is difficult to
describe verbally.

> Practice using pre-
sentation aids smooth-
ly and professionally.

> Have all materials
ready in advance.

> Don't use presentation
aids to cover up lack
of preparation or a
flat delivery style.

> Introduce presentation
aids so people have
some context for what
they're seeing or
hearing.

> Avoid blocking the
sight line between a
presentation aid and
your audience.

Web Sites

> Test the Internet access in the room where you
will be presenting. Determine if the connection is
fast enough to click through the site during your
presentation.

> Save the URL in your favorites file instead of
typing it in during the presentation. If you're
nervous, you might make mistakes and it could
throw off your concentration.

> Practice clicking through the site so you can
quickly get to the page you want. Write in your
notes the pathways you need.

> Visit the site on the day of your presentation to
see if the URL is still correct and all the links are
still current.

> Create screen shots that you can show in case
you can't access the Web site.

CHAPTER 5 ___ EXPRESSIVENESS

"You never get a second chance to make a good
first impression."
Will Rogers

First impressions count. Most people start evaluating whether they want to listen to you the minute they turn their attention to you. From your nonverbal actions, they assess your authority, confidence, attitude, and personality. They decide quickly whether you have something important to say.

Although it may not seem fair, nonverbal actions are like book covers. Even if the content is terrific, people may never read a book if the cover puts them off in some way. Verbal tics, distracting gestures, and a monotone delivery can prevent the audience from listening, even if they find the content valuable.

What are nonverbal actions? They are actions that the audience sees and sounds that the audience hears. The audience sees how you look and move, and they hear your voice, even if they're looking elsewhere in the room.

Why are nonverbal actions important? They are the strongest clue the audience has about your attitude toward the topic and your interest in it. They help the audience decide whether to take your ideas, information, and recommendations seriously. They also enhance a well-prepared presentation and make it memorable for the right reasons.

Do you know people who are animated in everyday conversations but clam up the minute they get in front of a group? Why is this so common? When some people get in front of a group, they become acutely self-conscious. They're nervous. They worry about being judged. They don't want to seem too enthusiastic, in case people don't agree with their ideas. They want an escape route. Other people think they are being expressive, but it doesn't come across to the audience. They believe they're being colorful and full of life, but they come across as black-and-white cardboard cutouts.

Whether you fit one of these descriptions or fall somewhere in between, you can learn how to use your natural expressiveness to your advantage during presentations. Most likely, you won't have to learn a whole new set of skills. You already have skills; it's just a matter of understanding them and using them to your advantage.

> ____ ATTITUDES

Attitude is difficult to fake or hide. If you aren't interested in your topic or feel ambivalent about what you're saying, people will pick up on your nonverbal clues. People will also mirror your attitude. If you're excited, they'll be interested. If you lack energy, they'll start to daydream.

What attitudes do you typically display about yourself, your topic, and your listeners? For example:

> aloof

> apologetic

> approachable

> arrogant

> bored

> condescending

> confident

> detached

> engaging

> enthusiastic

> halfhearted

> hesitant

> involved

> ironic

> nervous

> personable

> professional

> respectful

> ___ VISUAL FACTORS

What do people see when you give a presentation? They see you stand up, walk to the front of the room, and face the audience. They watch your gestures and assess how well you use presentation aids. If you stay seated, they see whether you hunch over or sit up straight. In either case, they pay attention to your face and register whether you're looking at them and are ready to interact.

Gestures and Movement

Movement attracts attention, which can be a positive or a negative experience for the presenter and the audience. If you move purposefully, the audience will view it as a seamless part of the presentation. If you move randomly, haphazardly, or repetitiously, they will be distracted. If you don't move at all, they'll wonder why you're so stiff.

Some people have a difficult time moving or gesturing while they present. They're like the Tin Man in *The Wizard of Oz*— they need some oil to help them move their creaky joints. If this describes you, don't worry. You won't be stuck in the forest forever, rusting away. There are things you can do!

First, assess how you typically move and gesture during a presentation. An excellent way to do this is to videotape yourself giving a presentation. If you're feeling brave, find some people to be your audience, even if you have to corral friends or family. It might feel awkward, but you will get a sense of how you typically act during a presentation. Review the tape to find both effective and ineffective behaviors:

> How is your posture?

> Do you balance your weight on both feet?

> Do you use nonverbal behaviors to emphasize key points?

> Do you have a variety of appropriate gestures?

> Are you rigid or relaxed?

> Do you overuse any actions or movements?

> Do you make random movements?

> Do you rock back and forth?

> Do you pace?

Seems basic, but how you stand can make a difference in how much energy you show and whether you can easily move to emphasize your points.

Try this exercise. Stand up and put your weight on one leg. Note that the weight is on the outside of your foot and on your heel. Now stand on both feet. Note that you are now putting the weight on the balls of your feet. This is your starting position. From this stance you can easily move in any direction to make a point. For example:

> Step forward when you're emphasizing a point or answering a question.

> Step back when you're completing a thought.

> Step from side to side when you use a comparison or show the contrast between two situations.

When people get nervous, they tend to clasp their hands, as if they were holding their own hands for support and comfort. They also fold their arms, put their hands behind their back, or put their hands in their pockets. Sometimes they're afraid their hands will shake or they'll gesture too much. Regardless of the reason, it inhibits their ability to gesture.

So what should you do with your hands? First, find a starting position from which you can comfortably gesture. Raise your arms straight out to both sides until they are at shoulder height. Then let them drop, bounce around, and come to a rest. Try this several times until you become comfortable. Note the location of your hands and arms. This is your starting position for gesturing.

The most common problem with hand and arm gestures is failing to give them sufficient strength and energy. Too often people use restrained or halfhearted gestures, which undermine their message.

Finish the gestures you begin to avoid distracting your audience. Use the "hold and follow through" technique: hold the gesture for a moment while you finish a statement, then drop the gesture.

Match your gestures to the room and the context. If you are in a large auditorium, use stronger, more expansive gestures. For example, move your arms from your shoulders instead of your elbows, take larger steps, or move across the stage.

Some people worry that they use the same gestures too often. Even though they want to try new gestures, they revert to their typical gestures when they get nervous. If this sounds familiar, don't despair! The secret is to change your focus. Instead of focusing on the gestures you want to do less frequently (which makes you think about them constantly), concentrate on the gestures that you want to use.

Increase your awareness of the types of gestures you could use. Pay attention to other presenters. Note the gestures they use and what they are talking about when they make those gestures. Also watch actors; they build their characters through nonverbal elements.

If you're worried about gestures, choreograph your presentation. Determine which gestures and movements will best support your key messages. During your practice sessions, exaggerate the gestures. Then, if you feel reticent or nervous during the presentation, you'll have muscle memory of the actions.

Increase your awareness of what gestures mean, especially if you're going to present in another country or to people from another culture. Nodding your head, moving your hand with the palm up or down, using one finger to point, waving—all have several meanings. For example, if you use the "V" sign with your index and middle finger in the United States, it stands for victory. In England, it can be a rude gesture.

Facial Expressions and Eye Contact

"The face you show the listener is the face that will look back at you."

We look for meaning in faces. We try to discern attitudes, feelings, and emotions. So it is especially important that your facial expressions reflect the tone of your message. Animation involves your entire face. It's a way to show energy through expressions and eye contact.

In every culture, facial expressions convey meaning. Of course, the same expressions mean different things in different cultures. Expressions convey subtleties and layers of meaning in addition to words. That's why travelers can be relatively successful at communicating when they speak only a few words of the local language. A few words plus several gestures can convey many messages.

A presenter who displays facial animation appears to be engaged with the issue and the audience. Conversely, a deadpan look conveys boredom and lack of conviction. What message do you wish to send?

Smiling is a key element of looking animated, but it has to be genuine. Real smiles indicate humor, warmth, irony, empathy, and so on. Halfhearted smiles look insipid, insincere, or anxious—none of which makes a positive impression.

We attach special meaning to the eyes. We say they are windows to the soul. We want to look at people's eyes to see if they're telling the truth. We can tell that a smile is genuine if the eyes are involved. When people avoid eye contact, there's a reason. They might feel unsure of themselves, nervous, or agitated. People also avoid eye contact with people they dislike, distrust, feel guilty about, or feel superior to. From this short list, you can see why eye contact is important.

At a minimum, make eye contact when you begin the presentation, when you emphasize a point, and when you end the presentation. "Fine," you might say, "I'll look up a few times. But I'm afraid that if I look up, I'll just stare and look like a deer in the headlights!"

Looking around the room is one antidote to staring. Look at an individual or a group of individuals until you come to a pause, a shift in emphasis, or some other transition. Then shift your view to another part of the room. The key here, as in many aspects of presentations, is balance. Just remember one thing: the area above people's heads is off-limits.

> ___ VOCAL EXPRESSION

When you give a presentation, your voice is the one nonverbal feature that is continually in use. It may seem illogical to think of your voice as a nonverbal feature, unless you think about sound instead of words. Listeners may glance away and not notice a facial expression, eye contact, or gesture, but they always hear your voice. Even if they wanted to, they can't shut it off.

A voice is more than the sum of its parts—but you need to understand the parts so that you can calibrate your voice to the occasion and the audience. It's like practicing sports or music: once you can perform the fundamentals well consistently, you'll be more effective when you play.

Articulation

Articulation refers to how clearly you form words. Many factors influence articulation, including habits, peer groups, the audience, and how quickly you're speaking. Depending on the individual or group, people expect presenters to speak a certain way. For example, we expect opera singers and pop singers to have different levels of articulation.

Sloppy articulation—dropping sounds within words or at the beginning or end of words—can make it difficult for people to understand you. It can also make you seem like you're speaking too quickly. To determine if you drop sounds, listen to how your friends and family speak; it's likely that you have a similar pattern. Then make a list of words with those letters or patterns, and practice saying them correctly. It will sound odd at first, but keep at it until it feels more natural.

Mispronunciation is related to sloppy articulation. If you habitually mispronounce common words or place the emphasis on the wrong syllable, it will grate on people's nerves. Start to pay attention to how newscasters pronounce words; they use standard pronunciation. Notice when they say a word differently than you do and try to emulate them. If you have questions, check a dictionary for pronunciation guidelines.

Inflection

Inflection is a rise or fall in pitch or volume to convey meaning. When someone says "What did you say?" it's the element that tells you whether that person is surprised, happy, shocked, angry, or depressed.

Inflection goes to the heart of what many presenters want to avoid: speaking in a monotone. As you know, a monotone means that you primarily use one pitch throughout the presentation. Which is monotonous!

If you find that you speak in a monotone, check to see what type of supporting material you are using. People often speak in a monotone while they give explanations. Adding examples, stories, quotations, or questions will naturally change your inflection: questions will raise your voice, a story will make you more animated, and a quote will cause you to pause.

How to practice inflection:

> Read plays and children's books aloud. Act out all the parts.

> Choose a paragraph to read. Then talk like a sports announcer, an auctioneer, a broadcaster, a teacher, a child, and so on. How does your inflection change?

> Practice saying the same phrase in several ways. For example, ask a question, make a statement, act uncertain, show surprise, display anger, convey confidence, express sadness.

> Do vocal gymnastics by reciting the alphabet or numbers. Go from your highest pitch to your lowest pitch, and back up to the highest. Don't strain your voice.

Pace

Pace refers to how quickly you speak. Like most people, you probably vary your pace during conversations. You rush when time is short and slow down when an idea is complicated or you want to emphasize it. Presenters usually do the same

Women often need to add lower pitches to their repertoire, and men often need to add higher pitches.

thing, unless they're nervous. Then they plow through their material as quickly as possible so they can get back to their seats and take a breath.

Viewing your presentation as a story can help. Storytellers use pace to make the story contract or expand, ebb and flow. They build suspense by accelerating their pace bit by bit.

Mix up the length of words and phrases to change your pace. Short words are quicker; long words cause you to slow down because it take time to pronounce them correctly.

Pauses are important components of pace. They're the "white space." Pauses are especially useful for transitions and emphasis. But too many pauses disrupt the momentum and continuity of a presentation.

People think faster than they can speak, which sometimes leads to words tumbling out helter-skelter. To become aware of your typical pace, build in real-time feedback during your practice session. Ask someone to signal you when you speak too rapidly. This will help you become more aware of your speaking rate.

Tape yourself talking, not reading, in several situations. If you practice while you're reading, you may slow down because you're unfamiliar with the material.

Quality

Resonant, full, high, low, colorful, scratchy, shrill, musical, nasal, airy, squeaky—what kind of voice do you have? Quality refers to the distinctive sound of a person's voice that makes it unique and recognizable. Musical instruments have distinct timbres—think of the difference between an oboe and a cello— and so do voices.

The quality of your voice affects an audience in several ways. Consider the voices you hear on radio or television commercials; they are chosen to convey an impression even before you listen to the words they say. For example, people find a resounding deep voice more credible and authoritative than a high, whiny voice.

The quality of your voice may vary. When you leave childhood, your voice deepens. If you're feeling emotional, you get choked up. Yelling, talking too long, or singing at the limits of your range makes you hoarse.

Develop awareness of where sound resonates (vibrates) when you speak. Do you feel the sound in your head, your throat, and your chest? Say "how-now-brown-cow" while you try to enlarge your mouth cavity to produce a rich tone. Feel the sound vibrate in your throat and chest, not just in your head.

Relax your face and neck. Let the air come through. Don't put your head down, which constricts your throat.

Volume and Projection

Some people can project to the back of a room without breaking a sweat. Others need to yell to be heard past the second row. What's the difference? Volume and projection, which are vocal elements that generate a sense of energy through audibility, intensity, and clarity.

People vary their volume for many reasons. Above all, it's boring to listen to someone speak at the exact same volume for an entire presentation. (Of course, it would be fascinating on some level to hear someone actually do this.) Also, consistent volume implies equality among your thoughts and messages, which prevents you from differentiating your key messages. Volume helps you emphasize words and concepts.

Many people forget that decreasing their volume is an option. A lower volume, combined with a pause, creates aural space for an idea.

Volume depends on the presenter's breath control. What happens when someone tells you to be aware of your breathing? Some people become so engrossed in their breathing pattern that they can't breathe normally anymore. When they're told

KEY POINTS TO REMEMBER

> Show consistency between your words and actions.

> Display your attitudes rather than say your attitudes.

> Movement attracts attention, so make sure your gestures have a purpose.

> Let gestures flow naturally from your message so you draw attention to the idea, not the gestures.

> Use facial animation to show that you are engaged with your audience.

> Develop the full potential of your voice.

> Use a variety of supporting material that varies your inflections.

> Craft key messages that you can say with one breath.

to breathe from their diaphragm, they start to take great gulps of air.

Breathing is something that happens naturally. Of course, this means that when you're in a stressful situation, your natural pattern will change. For example, you might begin to take shallow breaths, which will affect your ability to sustain your volume throughout phrases or sentences. The key is learning how to take normal breaths in a stressful situation, such as giving a presentation.

Become aware of your typical breathing pattern. Determine how many seconds you can speak with one breath. Then write key messages that you can say within that time period. This will help you work *with* your breathing pattern instead of against it. Take a note from composers of vocal, woodwind, and brass music. They know how long a musician can sustain a phrase, and they write accordingly.

CHAPTER 6 ___ QUESTIONS AND ANSWERS

The question-and-answer session is the part of a presentation that presenters look forward to the most, or dread the most, both for the same reason: unpredictability. Those who enjoy it tend to be quick thinkers who like the opportunity for give-and-take with an audience. They like to see if they can meet the challenge of unexpected questions.

Which is exactly what makes other people uneasy. They don't mind answering questions; they just wish they knew which questions they would be asked, so they could prepare. They prefer to have more time to craft their answers so they won't feel cornered or be bound to an answer that they made under pressure.

Context makes a big difference when it comes to asking and answering questions. In general, answering questions is a familiar interaction; most people field questions every day from their coworkers, family, friends, suppliers, customers, and other people. Their comfort level varies according to who is asking the questions and whether they know the answers.

Why should you improve your skills in this area? Whenever you work with people, you need to be able to communicate and clarify your message. Responding to questions is a basic communication tool that will help you during presentations and also give you confidence in other settings.

> ___ PREPARING FOR QUESTIONS

Anticipating questions and preparing answers takes away much of your "what if " anxiety. Prepare answers for several categories of questions:

> questions you expect people to ask you

> questions directly related to your key messages
  and supporting material

> questions about related issues

> questions related to the implications of your message

> questions you would like to answer

> questions for which there is no clear answer

In addition, practice what you will say if someone asks you a question for which you don't know the answer, or the issue is too complicated to get into during a 40-second answer. Write down several standard answers you can use to answer this type of question, so you can maintain control of the situation.

> ___ STARTING A QUESTION-AND-ANSWER SESSION

Imagine the following scenario: You have prepared for your presentation for three weeks. You have a list of 25 potential questions and airtight answers for each. You practiced answering hostile and aggressive questions, and you developed nonverbal actions that show your openness and confidence. There's only one problem: no one asks any questions.

Sometimes people are reluctant to ask questions, and you need to get them started. Here are some techniques you can use:

> Announce that there will be a Q&A session at the end of your presentation, and indicate how long it will last.

> Let people know that you will take five to ten minutes to provide some background on an issue, then answer their questions.

> Hand out cards or paper for people to write questions.

> Say, "I'd be happy to respond to any questions you have."

> Start with one of your own questions. For example, "One of the questions I often hear about this topic (problem, issue, concern) is . . . "

> Begin with a question that emphasizes a key message or expands on information you covered in your key messages.

> Ask two or three colleagues who will be in the audience to get the questions started.

> ___ ANSWERING QUESTIONS

The following guidelines will help you appear confident and calm as you field questions.

Pause to think. Before you answer a question, pause for a moment. Make sure you understand both the substance of the question and the intent of the questioner. Otherwise, you may give an answer that is literally correct but ignores the broader issue.

People try to buy time by saying "That's a good question." Unfortunately, this phrase has become a cliché. Many listeners find it irritating and condescending. Or they may feel offended if you term several questions "good" but don't say anything about *their* questions. Also, some presenters use this phrase so consistently that they call questions good even when they're irrelevant or poorly phrased.

Instead of making a value judgment about a question (good or great), use a descriptive term, such as "complicated," "apt," "insightful," or "difficult."

Speak to the entire audience. Look at the person who asked the question at the beginning and end of your answer. During the answer, speak to the entire audience, not just to one person or one area of the room.

Be honest. It's tempting to be the expert on every facet of your topic, even if you need to bluff in order to do it—but you know how this will end. The minute you get caught, your credibility will plummet. The only way to prevent this is to admit when you don't know the answer to a question. If someone in the audience can answer the question better, invite that person to respond. Otherwise (if it's appropriate), offer to track down the answer and convey it to the questioner and the group.

Develop a sense of timing. Try an experiment. (You may want to ask a friend to help you.) Look at your watch or a clock. When the second hand reaches 12, close your eyes. Keep your eyes closed for 20 seconds, or for what you think is 20 seconds. No counting allowed! Open your eyes. How much time actually passed?

Developing your temporal sense can help you answer questions more effectively. Research and experience indicate that answers of 10 to 40 seconds are the most effective. If you develop a sense of how long 20 to 30 seconds is when you're speaking, you can give answers that are neither abrupt nor too elaborate.

Practice answering questions while you use a stopwatch or a watch with a second hand. Write down 10 questions about your topic on cards, select one at random, and give a 30-second answer.

Repeat the question only if necessary. Repeat the question only if you want to make sure that everyone heard it, or if you want to clarify the question before you answer it. Routinely repeating questions may give the impression that you are stalling, which can annoy listeners.

Answer concisely. Many presenters obscure their answers by using a "funnel" structure. They dump statistics, explanations, examples, and other material into the top of the funnel, which swirls around and around until the answer comes out the bottom. For example, "Thanks for asking that question . . . according to research . . . we've thought about it this way . . . and that's why we decided to make this decision at this time." As you can imagine, when a presenter uses this answer structure, people often quit listening before they hear the answer.

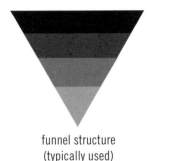

funnel structure
(typically used)

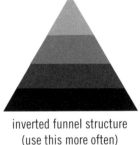

inverted funnel structure
(use this more often)

To fix this, simply turn the structure upside down—use an inverted funnel structure. Instead of starting with the explanation, start with the answer. Then use an example, statistic, comparison, or explanation to back it up. In other words, put the answer in the narrow end of the funnel, then let it expand.

For example, pretend you're giving a presentation about how your group is going to be more responsive to customers, and you're now taking questions. Someone asks if you're going to do anything to decrease the amount of time that it takes to process an invoice. Instead of immediately explaining how you're going to change the process, begin with "Yes, we plan to decrease the average time it takes to process it by 50 percent or more. Here is how."

You can also use the inverted funnel structure when you answer lengthy or multifaceted questions. It will help you avoid the appearance of stalling, or ducking a question. Divide the question into parts, and answer each part in turn, using the inverted funnel. Monitor people's reactions to your answers. If it seems necessary, ask them if they would like you to comment further.

Even though you're using the inverted funnel structure to expand on your answer, don't view it as an opportunity to speak as long as you'd like. Limit yourself to a 40 to 45-second answer, or your audience will think you're launching into another presentation.

Watch for reactions. As you answer questions, monitor the reactions of both the questioner and the audience. If listeners seem confused, restate your point with an example or explanation. If people nod affirmatively, continue. Don't belabor a point if the audience seems to understand you.

Keep on track. Tangents cause you to slide off the topic and get stuck in unrelated topics and opinions. To avoid this, be clear about your key messages. Then you can recognize connections between seemingly tangential questions and your key messages, and adroitly combine them.

The audience may show more energy and interest in the tangent than in your topic. If people insist on talking about the tangent, offer to discuss it after the presentation is over or to hold another discussion devoted solely to that topic.

Later, analyze their motivation for discussing the tangent. Why did it spark their interest? Perhaps it was more relevant to their daily work, or it involved information that was more compelling. Or perhaps you showed more interest in this topic, and they responded to your enthusiasm.

Stay on schedule. End the presentation on time. You will retain the goodwill of your listeners, and that of any presenters following you. Offer to talk after the presentation with individuals who have more questions.

Provide a capper. Questions, even though they may be compelling, can pull you off your key messages. This means you run the risk of ending your session on an unrelated or peripheral topic. To avoid this, use a capper. A capper is an improvised and abbreviated conclusion in which you restate your key messages, your final emphasis, and/or your implication statement. It should take about 10 to 30 seconds. By using a capper, you can take advantage of the "recency effect": listeners remember best what you say last.

In chapter 3, we used the following example to illustrate key messages. Here is how it could be used in a capper.

A presenter stated that in his experience:

> Effective leaders demonstrate vision.

> Effective leaders demonstrate integrity.

> Effective leaders demonstrate patience.

> Effective leaders demonstrate persistence.

> Effective leaders demonstrate passion.

During the discussion, an audience member mentioned that innovation was also important to leadership success in the industry, so the presenter included that concept in this capper:

> Not only are vision and passion important qualities for our leaders, but innovative thinking is also important. Our challenge is to learn, find, and create additional ways to lead with vision, innovation, and passion.

Note that the capper includes a partial summary, the addition of "innovation," and a general implication statement.

> ___ HANDLING AGGRESSIVE QUESTIONS

Aggressive questions can be unsettling. They can make you feel angry, frustrated, defensive, or even panicked.

Hostile, aggressive, or emotional questions are always multi-layered, consisting of a substantive issue and an emotional overtone or undertone. When you receive one, follow these guidelines. They will help you defuse the situation and give the questioner a substantive answer.

Maintain control. First, keep your own emotions in check. Resist being defensive or thinking of the question as a personal attack. Take a deep breath and show an appropriate facial expression. Focus on understanding the person's question rather than on how you feel about the question. This will help you convey confidence and control as you answer the question.

Lower your voice level to convey command of your emotions. Avoid laughing at a question. Even a nervous laugh is likely to be misinterpreted.

Empathize with the questioner. People who ask aggressive or hostile questions are caught up in the emotion of an issue. They want you to understand how they feel about it. Until they have a sense that you comprehend the underlying emotion, they won't be interested in your information. In fact, if you launch into a calm, logical answer, it could make them more aggressive.

To determine the questioner's emotions, listen for words that indicate feelings: happy, sad, worried, upset, annoyed. Also watch for nonverbal clues—facial expressions, gestures, vocal intensity—to the questioner's mood.

Use a reflective statement to show that you understand that this is an issue the questioner feels strongly about. Reflective statements are short declarative sentences that acknowledge emotions or feelings. They help you create rapport and show that you understand the questioner's emotions.

Rephrase the question. After showing empathy, rephrase the question in neutral terms. This will help you move from the emotional aspect of the question to the substantive issue. Briefly restate the question to show that you understand the substantive issue, problem, or concern. Phrase the question simply and, if you can, positively. If that is difficult or awkward, reframe the question as a more complex or multifaceted issue.

Answer the question. Answer the neutrally rephrased question. Consider using the inverted funnel technique so that you can address the issue immediately, then expand on your answer.

Create a bridge to related content. Sometimes the questioner may not be familiar with all aspects of the situation. This is an opportunity for you to move into related information that will broaden and enrich your answer.

Deal with objections immediately. If people object to your statements or contradict them, respond immediately. If you ignore the challenge, they may be convinced that the objections are more valid than your key messages.

Build on supportive statements. When people support your position, reinforce their comments. Affirm and comple-ment their statements.

> ___ PANEL DISCUSSIONS

Question-and-answer sessions come in several forms. We have spent this chapter talking about situations in which you handle all questions yourself. Before we go, we want to add a few tips on other formats, in which you answer questions as a member of a group or moderate a panel discussion.

When you answer questions as a member of a group, follow these tips:

> Open the discussion with a comment such as, "Now it's time to get your comments and ques-tions on this issue. We invite you to address your questions to an individual or to the group at large."

> Briefly explain the ground rules and process, including how long the question period will last.

> Depending on the logistics, ask people to stand up when they answer a question and sit down when they finish.

> Let other people finish their sentences before you jump in.

> Monitor how often you answer questions compared to the other people in the group. Try not to dominate the session.

When you moderate a panel discussion, consider the following suggestions:

> Learn about the people on the panel. Become familiar with their expertise so you can direct appropriate questions toward them.

> Inform everyone on the panel of the guidelines for the discussion: how long the session will last, how many minutes each person gets to answer a question, whether they will have a chance to add to their answers later.

> Be conscious of time.

> Prepare phrases you can use to move on to the next question, especially if an answer is going on too long. ("I would like to explore this further after the session. Let's move on so we have time to address several questions in the time we have left.")

> Keep the group focused on the purpose of the discussion. The audience wants to learn something. They don't want to listen to panelists talk about tangents.

> Use a capper to sew up a discussion. Take approximately 30 to 60 seconds to repeat some key messages and to emphasize an area of common ground (priorities, values) that you share with the audience.

> Use two-thirds of your time to deliver your presentation and one-third to answer questions.

> Know how to get a question-and-answer session started.

> Use an inverted funnel structure to answer questions.

> Answer questions honestly.

> Don't belabor a point if the audience understands you.

> Stay on track; avoid tangents.

> Resist viewing aggressive questions as personal attacks.

> Use a capper to end a question-and-answer session.

CHAPTER 7 —— BUILDING YOUR CONFIDENCE

Fear is the number one reason why people avoid giving presentations. So why don't we call this chapter "conquering your fear" instead of "building confidence"? Because we believe it's unrealistic to focus on eradicating your fear. Instead, we want you to harness that fear and use it to your advantage. We want to turn your fear inside out and transform it into confidence.

Confidence springs from competence and commitment. Confidence is also a force behind success. When you feel confident, you take risks that stretch your natural abilities. When you succeed, you feel competent, which increases your confidence even more.

Nervousness about giving a presentation to a group (also known as stage fright, speech anxiety, or communication apprehension) is a form of anticipatory anxiety. Thinking about having to speak in front of other people triggers symptoms like butterflies in the stomach, cold and clammy hands, a dry mouth, weak knees, light-headedness, a racing heart. Ironically, a person with stage fright experiences physiological effects similar to those experienced by a person who is stimulated by an audience—they just reframe their symptoms and use their energies differently. Fearful presenters hold their tension inside, where it becomes a distraction, while confident presenters direct their tension into the presentation and use it to show energy, animation, and conviction.

> ___ PRESENTATION ANXIETY

Most presenters feel some anxiety when they get up in front of an audience. Before you give your next presentation, read this list.

> Most presenters, even experienced professionals, experience some measure of nervousness.

> The presence of anxiety shows that you are moving out of your comfort zone and attempting to learn and grow. You are refusing to become stagnant.

> Anticipation is nearly always worse than reality.

> Anxiety is raw material for an energetic, animated presentation. It just has to be shaped and channeled in the right direction.

> Anxiety is not as noticeable to listeners as it is to the presenter. Listeners are usually empathetic and understanding if you show a little nervousness; they know how it feels to be up in front of a group.

> The intensity of anxiety decreases as you become more experienced, but it doesn't disappear.

> You can do something about presentation anxiety—start giving presentations. Begin small and work your way up. Never pass up opportunities to practice.

> ___ DEVELOPING YOUR CONFIDENCE

OK, so you've decided to face your fears and give a presentation. Now what? Here are tips and techniques to help you feel prepared and relatively relaxed.

The weeks before the presentation	The day of the presentation	During the presentation
> Visualization > Positive thinking > Content preparation > Videotaped rehearsal > Feedback and adjustments > Rehearsal in room or auditorium	> Visualization > Positive thinking > Tension-release exercises > Comfortable, professional clothes > The right food and beverages > Rapport building with audience	> Deep breathing > Focus on the audience > Awareness of the audience and ability to adjust to their needs > Ability to handle problems smoothly

> ___ THE WEEKS BEFORE THE PRESENTATION

Depending on the presentation, your preparation time may vary from a few hours to a few months. Regardless of the amount of time you have, the activities in this section will help you lay the foundation for increased confidence.

Visualization and Positive Thinking

Visualization and positive thinking go hand in hand. Visualization is picturing the physical setting and your experience in giving a presentation. It includes rehearsing how you will handle difficult people or issues.

What is positive thinking? It's the little voice in your head that says you will do well because you're prepared, capable, and energized to share your message with the audience. We're not talking about that nagging little voice that says you'll never be able to do it because _____ (fill in the blank with your favorite self-doubt).

Become aware of your inner dialogue, or the messages you typically send yourself through your "inner critic." Each time you criticize yourself, substitute a positive message. For example, replace "I always use the same gestures" with "I'm going to add one new gesture the next time I speak."

When you have a few minutes, try this visualization exercise:
Imagine yourself giving an effective presentation. Picture the room, the audience, and your position in the room. Focus on each section of your presentation—the walk to the front of the room, your opening line, each key point, your conclusion, and the walk back to your seat. Don't forget the thunderous applause at the end.

When you have more time, use this version:
Sit down in a quiet place where you won't be disturbed. Close your eyes. Take a deep breath and let it out. Imagine the place where you will give the presentation: the walls, the chairs, the tables, and the colors and shapes. When you have the scene clear in your mind, describe yourself giving a strong, well-prepared presentation.

"I walk to the front of the room, look at the audience, and smile. I pause for a moment to take a deep breath. I begin talking in a firm, strong voice. I speak in a controlled, clear, and pleasant manner. As I make eye contact with individual members of my audience, I notice that they are paying close attention and some are smiling. I feel relaxed and at ease. I'm having a good time. I know my material and enjoy talking about it with the audience."

Now imagine someone very different from you getting up and delivering your presentation. Pick someone you know who is older or younger than you, or of the opposite gender. Imagine that person being a little nervous at first, but then delivering your presentation in a relaxed, natural manner. See the smiling, applauding audience. Run through this scene twice, seeing this person struggling, then succeeding.

Next, imagine an acquaintance giving your presentation. Choose someone who is the same age, gender, and general appearance as you. Picture this person being a little nervous, but then getting into it and doing an excellent job. Run through this scene twice.

Finally, imagine the same scene with you giving the presentation. You're a little hesitant at first, but then you gain confidence and speak with authority and energy. You make a few mistakes but handle them smoothly. By the end the audience is genuinely pleased and you feel great. Run through this scene until you feel your confidence increase.

Preparation and Practice

Some people merely glance at their notes before speaking in front of 500 people. Other people need to practice their presentations seven or eight times before they feel comfortable, even when they're speaking to only a few people. The key is doing what *you* need to do to feel prepared.

Preparation is the foundation of confidence. When you know your topic, including its unique angles and quirks, you're ready to discuss it, answer questions, and convey a clear message. On the other hand, if you are unprepared, you *should* be nervous!

One effective way to practice is to videotape your presentation. Force yourself to go through the entire thing; don't skip around or stop in the middle if you make a mistake. Then review the tape and assess your nonverbal behaviors, including your gestures, eye contact, and facial expressions. Pay attention to your voice: volume, pace, clarity, intonation. Pinpoint where you can use shorter words and sentences, or use more precise language. Scrutinize where your transitions are unclear and where you should repeat a phrase, or add or delete detail.

Next, ask an experienced presenter to review the tape with you and point out areas where you are doing well and areas where you need improvement. Ask for targeted feedback. Check to see if the person understood your key messages. It may be painful, but it's much better to get the feedback now than to hear it after your "real" presentation.

If you were dissatisfied with what you saw on the tape, decide what you want to change. Be specific. For example, you may decide that you need to speak more rapidly or use different gestures. Videotape yourself again after making these changes. Continue to experiment and fine-tune until you are comfortable with your presentation.

If you can arrange it, rehearse your presentation in the room or auditorium where you will be presenting. Ask some colleagues to join you, and have them sit in different sections of the room: front, middle, back, each side. Invite them to tell you if they can't see the visuals or can't hear you, or if you need to adjust your presentation in some other way to make it more appropriate for the room. This will also give you a chance to see if the equipment works properly.

> ___ THE DAY OF THE PRESENTATION

The big day has arrived! You thought you were calm until you woke up this morning. Now you wish you had looked up one more statistic, videotaped yourself one more time, or taken a different suit to the cleaners.

This is the day when all your preparation is going to pay off. Of course you feel nervous—it's part of the event. Although it may not help to hear this, there would be something wrong if you didn't feel nervous. You've done all the preparation; you're ready.

Remember that you are communicating, not performing.

Resist looking over your presentation notes during the last two hours before you speak. Looking at them repeatedly will make you more nervous, not less. You may also start to tinker with the presentation. Instead, use this time to meet some members of the audience. Building rapport will settle your nerves and give you some friendly faces to look for while you present. If this is not an option, use the time to do positive visualization and relaxation exercises. Focus on something other than your presentation.

Clothing and Appearance

Being in control of your visual image—feeling comfortable and knowing you look good—will bolster your self-confidence and help you relax. Wear an outfit that you look good in, one that allows you to stand, sit, and move freely. Avoid pants, jackets, belts, or skirts that are too tight, heels that are too high, skirts that are too short. As a general rule, don't wear an outfit for the first time. You may feel self-conscious in it, and it may surprise you in a way you aren't prepared for: the pants may crease when you sit down, or the jacket may be difficult to gesture in.

If you're not sure what to wear, call ahead to the event coordinator. Or dress up a notch from what you expect. Never dress too casually.

Dealing with Tension

To become aware of where tension affects your body, deliberately tense and relax various parts of your body. Starting with your shoulders, go down your arms, torso, upper legs, lower legs, feet, and toes. Then go back up your body again. Tense each muscle group for three to five seconds, then relax for three to five seconds.

Just before your presentation, relax your whole body. Go through this relaxation procedure twice: Sit in a comfortable position. Pull your feet and toes up, tightening your shins. Hold for five seconds and relax. Curl your toes, tighten your calves, thighs, and buttocks. Hold for five seconds, then relax for ten seconds. Notice the relaxation flooding your legs.

Clench both fists, tightening your forearms and biceps. Hold for five seconds, then relax for ten seconds. Notice the wave of relaxation that goes through your arms. Repeat this once or twice.

Arch your back slightly as you take a deep breath. Hold for five seconds. Relax and exhale. Take another deep breath, drawing the breath down into your abdomen. Hold five seconds and relax for ten seconds. Notice the relaxation in your chest and abdomen. Repeat this breathing pattern up to five times; it will help you feel more relaxed and invigorated.

Tilt your head back, roll it clockwise in a complete circle, and then counterclockwise. Now contract the muscles in your face: wrinkle up your forehead, frown, squint your eyes, purse your lips, press your tongue against the roof of your mouth. Hold the contraction of each small muscle group for five seconds and relax for ten seconds. Notice the relaxation in the many small muscles of your head.

Before you start speaking, take a slow deep breath and let it out gradually. Besides being the best way to relax quickly, this will fill your lungs fully before you speak. You can also pause and take a deep breath to relax at any time during your presentation. To your listeners, it will seem like a natural pause.

> ___ THE PRESENTATION

This is it. You're in the room listening to the introduction. Now your name is announced. It's time to walk up to the lectern, or take the microphone, or simply start talking. Why is your voice so squeaky? Can everyone hear your heart pounding? You thought you were relaxed but now it seems like you can't get a breath. And everyone is staring at you, seemingly impatient for you to start talking.

Whoa! Stop the negative thinking. You're going to be fine. You rehearsed, relaxed, visualized, and prepared—you're ready. Start with a strong opening. Know exactly what you want to say. Getting off to a good start helps dissipate anxiety. Then focus on your message and on the audience. This will divert your attention from your own anxiety. To do this, think about moving through the following three circles.

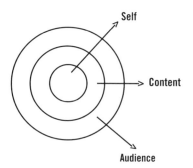

If you're just starting to give presentations, you're probably in the innermost circle. You mainly focus on how you sound and look. If you have some experience, you're probably in the middle circle, where you focus on content and your delivery. If you have been giving presentations for some time, you're probably in the outermost circle. Your confidence regarding your delivery and your ability to choose and sequence content gives you freedom to focus on your listeners.

When you become nervous, think about moving out at least one circle. If you start to focus on yourself, think of your content. If you're worried about your content, focus on the audience.

Getting Flustered

fluster: a state of agitated confusion

Sometimes, no matter how much you prepare, things go wrong. In all likelihood, the presentation won't go exactly as planned. You may have to cut some material, a question may take more of your time than you expected, or a key person may not be in the audience. Fight against the feeling that unless every detail goes perfectly, the presentation is a failure. Insisting on controlling every aspect of the presentation will cause you a great deal of frustration, which will add to your anxiety.

Remember that most people are looking for information, not perfection. They want to be reasonably engaged in your presentation and will forgive mistakes as long as you are prepared.

Memorization can help you get through rough patches. Memorize your introduction, transitions, and conclusion. When you reach these spots, they will be familiar and you can mentally relax for a moment. But don't memorize your entire presentation. We have seen people regret doing this, because they get completely lost if they miss one sentence.

Losing Your Place

A color-coded outline can help you keep track of where you are in your presentation. Using highlighter markers, choose one color for key messages, a second color for supporting material, and a third color for the conclusion. This will help you quickly locate your place.

If you lose your place during the presentation, try one of the following techniques:

> Give a quick summary of what you have covered so far, and a preview of what you will talk about next.

> Redirect attention away from you by asking a question of the audience. Bring along a card on

which you have written two or three questions you can use at any point in your presentation.

> Make a brief comment, pause to look at your notes, and continue with your presentation. For example, "In my excitement I may have gotten a little ahead of myself, so let me be sure I haven't skipped anything vital."

> Resist saying "I get so nervous presenting." Listeners will begin looking for telltale signs, real or imagined.

> Try to interject a bit of humor.

> ___ ADAPTABILITY

Presenters face a paradox: they need to be prepared and in control of their content and delivery, yet they also need to be flexible and responsive to the situation. How can they do this?

Think back to the three circles we mentioned earlier: self, content, and audience. Presenters who focus primarily on themselves have a harder time adapting to the circumstances. They might not notice that the situation has changed, or they may become hooked on the idea that the situation shows that they weren't prepared enough. A common reaction is to become too serious or subdued. The presenter backs off, then the audience backs off, which makes the presenter back off more, and so on.

When presenters focus on their content, they are more adaptable. Because they are so familiar with their content, they can readily decide what is necessary and what is optional, and can cut material as they go. Many people mark sections that could be easily cut and put in transition words that help them do this smoothly.

> Anticipation is nearly
always worse than
reality.

> Anxiety is not as
noticeable to
listeners as it is to
the presenter.

> Preparation is the
foundation of confi-
dence. Do what you
need to do to feel
prepared.

> Visualize yourself
giving a successful
presentation.

> Learn a relaxation
technique and
practice it before
your presentation.

> Have a conversation
with the audience.
You are communi-
cating, not performing.

> Get off to a good start
to dissipate anxiety.

> Remember that the
audience is looking
for information, not
perfection.

People who focus on the audience are the most adaptable. Watching for audience cues, they're able to recognize when people need more or less information, or when they're not interested, or when everything is going well. They're in the moment. They're having a conversation with the audience, and they're enjoying themselves.

Adaptability is not restricted to the most experienced pre-senters; anyone can reach this level. Your adaptability is bound to ebb and flow according to the situation, but expecting that things will change will help you to prepare and to respond appropriately.

CHAPTER 8 ___ STYLE

When you hear the word *style*, two thoughts probably spring to your mind. You wonder whether you have a style (you do), and you wonder whether you can swap your style for someone else's (you can't). To your delight or dismay, your presentation style reflects you—your voice, language, mannerisms, appearance, preferences, and humor, and the way you interact with others.

Style plays a role in every presentation, whether it's a quick five-minute update at a meeting or an hour-long speech at a convention. Style is not something you create for an occasion; it's something you tailor to an occasion. Style is also a catchall word. It refers to broad categories and small details, covering everything from what you wear and the language you use to the format of the presentation and the formality of the occasion.

In this chapter, we're going to talk about style in two contexts. First, we'll talk about your personal style. Then we'll talk about how to adjust your style to fit the audience, the topic, and the situation.

> ___ PERSONAL STYLE

Defined simply, your personal style is how you present yourself. Your style consists of several elements combined in a unique whole. The elements include:

> appearance and dress

> physicality (stance and posture; movement; gesture frequency, size, and extent)

> communication patterns

> vocal inflections, patterns, pace, quality

> language, words, and syntax (phrases, slang, jargon)

> type and frequency of interaction

Every person has a default style, shaped by personality, environment, experiences, communication preferences, and other factors. While your style reflects how you typically act or prefer to act, it's not an immutable limit. You have the ability to adjust it to the situation. Note that we say adjust, not alter.

> ___ IDENTIFYING YOUR STYLE

One effective way to identify your style is to videotape two or more of your presentations in different settings. Seeing yourself on tape is the best way to get a sense of your mannerisms, energy, and overall demeanor. This will give you an idea of whether and how to adjust your style to fit the circumstances.

You can also seek feedback from audience members. The next time you give a presentation, ask two or three people if they would be willing to give you feedback on your style. When you meet, listen graciously (no defensive comments), and thank each person for the feedback. If they talk about other aspects of your presentation, try not to get frustrated. Ask a few clarifying questions. Later, analyze the comments and pull out some themes.

Reflect on descriptions and phrases people have made about your presentation skills. Most likely your style has been generally consistent, and you can get a fairly accurate picture from their comments. For example:

> Casual: You prefer to improvise rather than prepare. You count on the audience to ask a lot of questions.

> Precise: You do a lot of preparation and stick close to your outline or script. You don't want any surprises.

> High energy: You talk fast, gesture a lot, and may try to cover more information than you can cover within the allotted time.

> Lighthearted: You use a lot of humor and are uncomfortable if things get too serious.

> ___ GETTING OUT OF YOUR OWN WAY

Most of us don't think about our style as we interact with people throughout the day. We make slight adjustments as needed, because we have learned the unspoken rules for navigating in professional and social situations. But many of us don't take advantage of that knowledge when we give presentations. We convince ourselves that the unspoken rules of presentations are different, and more difficult. We focus so much on ourselves that we suppress our natural style.

Of course, that's a common reaction when several pairs of eyes are focused exclusively on you. Even if you enjoy being the center of attention, it can be intimidating to give a presentation. Your challenge as a presenter may be to get out of your own way.

A common style issue concerns lack of movement, which may make you seem robotic. Here is a simple exercise you can do to improve in this area. For the next week, pay attention to your gestures, your movements, and your level of animation in everyday conversations with your friends and coworkers. Compare this to how you act when you give presentations. When do you pull back? What do you quit doing? What vocal expressiveness do you subdue?

Check to see if you're doing these actions:

voice   monotone, flat, little energy, no difference in pace, lack of intonation

face   minimal eye contact with audience, the same facial expression throughout (deadpan)

gestures little or no use of gestures—or quick, rigid, staccato movements

movement riveted to one place

Sometimes presenters make up for lack of movement with an outpouring of words. Check to see if your verbal style includes any of these behaviors:

> Using qualifiers and intensifiers, or repeating a word. You might think they will make a statement stronger, but they have the opposite effect. For example, "We really had a very, very, very productive meeting. Just a great meeting." It would be more effective to say, simply, "We had a productive meeting."

> Speaking like a writer. Writers can get away with complex sentences; speakers can't. If you simplify your sentences, they will automatically become shorter and easier to understand.

> Using broad language. It might be more fun to say *precipitation* than *rain*, but it's not as specific. Focus on finding exact words instead of getting in the general vicinity. For example, which would you rather hear: "The client appreciated our work" or "Our work with their team didn't just

help them—it transformed the way they performed. They have been more effective, efficient, and productive ever since. In fact, productivity is up over 60 percent."

Presenters may use a verbal style that makes them appear uncertain. If you feel like audiences don't take you seriously, check for these behaviors:

> Frequently discount your words or hedge with phrases like "I think," "maybe," "sort of," "perhaps," and "I guess." When you use these phrases, you appear to lack conviction and confidence.

> Raise your voice at the end of declarative sentences. If you always sound like you're asking questions, it will never sound like you're giving answers. A few years ago, teenagers and twenty-somethings talked like this all the time, which tended to annoy their older colleagues. Besides causing generational tension, it can also make you sound hesitant or tentative.

> ___ ASSESSING YOUR STYLE

A personal presentation style can help you or hurt you, depending on the context. As you prepare your presentation, think about how people might react to your style. Here are some examples:

Style	Help	Hindrance
animated	entertains an audience	could seem incongruous when you're delivering serious messages
casual	puts people at ease, good for highly interactive presentations	doesn't work as well with individuals who don't want instant rapport, may seem less professional
charismatic	sweeps audience along, holds them rapt	audience may be suspicious, wonder if there's substance beneath the surface
confrontational	able to address tough issues	could come on too strong
didactic	effective for highly detailed explanations	risks being boring, flat, too detailed
engaging	audience feels involved	too folksy in some settings
formal	works well in structured, one-way communication	hinders interaction
humorous	puts people at ease, audience often enjoys content more	could detract from weight of message, may not appear serious about topic, may use inappropriate humor
ironic	reveals layers of meaning, finds wry humor in difficult situations	risks sounding cynical or sarcastic
neutral	effective in volatile situations	could seem noncommittal
no-nonsense	appears trustworthy, no hidden agenda	may lack finesse, especially in situations that require nuance
reserved	no false enthusiasm	may have difficulty connecting with an audience; may appear to lack conviction and passion
self-effacing	makes the message more prominent than the presenter	may seem to lack authority and confidence

> ___ ADJUSTING YOUR STYLE

Tailor your style when your actions or language could undermine or overshadow your message. As you consider potential adjustments to your style, remember that less is often more. Make subtle changes. You are giving a presentation to convey information, not to practice using different styles. If you make drastic changes in your style, people who know you will be puzzled and distracted, and will wonder why you're acting like this. People who don't know you will sense that something is slightly askew, since you probably won't be successful at sustaining the style change throughout the presentation.

To decide what to adjust, answer these questions:

1. What is your typical style?

2. What is the style of the occasion?

3. What would be most appropriate for the setting?

4. Are there gaps between your typical style and what would be appropriate?

5. What could you adjust in order to be more effective?

> ___ MATCHING YOUR STYLE TO THE OCCASION

Every type of presentation has a set of expectations regarding format, style, and tone. It is to your advantage to match your style to the occasion. Presentations fall somewhere on these three continuums:

Formality: formal ⟵⟶ informal

Interaction: minimal ⟵⟶ high level

Tone: serious ⟵⟶ lighthearted

These three areas are often connected. For example, formal presentations tend to be more serious and unidirectional; informal presentations tend to be more interactive and humorous. Let's look at each area in more detail.

Formality

Some presentations are obviously formal: State of the Union addresses, keynote addresses, commencement speeches, academic and professional lectures, religious services, recognition banquets. In a formal presentation, here's what you can expect:

> The presenter almost always stands.

> The presenter reads from a script, or uses a TelePrompTer extensively.

> The material is often arranged according to a standard format.

> There is little or no interaction with the audience, and no expectation of discussion.

> The presenter has time to develop elaborate metaphors, analogies, and stories.

> The presenter may rely heavily on explanations, quotes, and statistics.

> There is little or no use of slang.

> The information is also aimed at an audience beyond those in the room.

> Members of the news media may attend the presentation.

> There may be an understanding that the presentation will be studied and parsed; it may become part of a historical record.

Informal presentations fall at the other end of the spectrum. Some examples are staff meetings, team updates, and classroom discussions. In this type of presentation:

> The presenter may sit or stand.

> The audience and presenter expect to interact.

> The presentation is a catalyst for dialogue, discussion, and debate.

> The presenter uses several short anecdotes and examples.

> The presenter rarely uses a unifying metaphor that requires time to develop.

If you have a choice, how formal should you be? It depends on the atmosphere you want to create and the purpose of your presentation. If you're trying to create a collaborative atmosphere, be less formal. (This is often a good choice in a business setting.) If you want to convey a message but not solicit comments or have a discussion, be more formal.

Interaction

An interactive style invites the audience to participate in the presentation. You draw them in and ask them to be more than passive listeners. The dynamics of a presentation change when the presenter involves listeners. Listeners feel like the presenter is talking *with* them, rather than *at* them.

There are no hard and fast rules for incorporating interaction into a presentation. It depends on the audience, your purpose, the setting, the logistics, and your comfort level.

Asking questions is one of the best ways to involve the audience. You can ask questions in groups of any size, in both formal and informal situations. People respond most readily to questions about their experiences, preferences, expertise, and opinions on a public issue. For example: "How many of you have experienced poor customer service? (Pause for a show of hands.) What was that experience like?"

Some presenters get "dead air" because they ask the wrong kinds of questions. Here are some mistakes you may have seen:

> Questions that are too general. Listeners aren't sure what they're being asked.

> Questions that call for specific information. Listeners may not know the correct answer and don't want to look ignorant.

> Questions about personal or private matters. Listeners might be unwilling to talk about these matters in a public setting.

If you want your presentation to be interactive, you have to be willing to take charge of the situation. You're managing the experience for the audience. It's your responsibility to decide when and how to involve the audience, keep people on topic, draw disparate thoughts together, play off the ideas and energy of the listeners, and, in the midst of it all, convey a coherent message.

This may sound similar to facilitating a meeting. But the differences are:

> You play a larger role than you would as facilitator of a meeting.

> You are the primary presenter.

> It's your agenda rather than a shared agenda.

> You have more control; you can pull back and limit interaction if it's disruptive.

> People are less likely to interrupt you to pursue their own agenda.

Tone

Presenters who strike the right tone align their words and actions with the purpose of the presentation and the expectations of the audience. They understand the nuance of a gesture, the connotation of a phrase, and the value of well-timed humor.

To determine what tone you should use, consider the formality of the occasion. For example, if you're talking about a current controversy in your industry, you will probably strike a more serious tone than if you were speaking at a celebration banquet. Also consider your audience's expectations. Determine where they fall on the continuum between substantive information delivered in a sober manner and attention-grabbing information delivered in an entertaining way.

Aim for a consistent tone. If you mix your tone too much—serious one moment, humorous the next—people won't know what to expect or what to believe. They might assume that you're making light of a serious situation or diminishing its importance. At times, though, you may want to shift your tone to break tension, or to make a serious point in a humorous way.

Effective presenters consistently come across as both personable and professional. Humor helps convey your personable side and is one of the primary tools for setting the tone of your presentation. Used well, humor helps create a favorable impression. Used poorly, it can leave a negative impression that overshadows your message.

To use humor effectively, try these suggestions:

> Collect several types of humorous content that you can use in presentations. Include quips, phrases, quotations, anecdotes, and cartoons.

> Choose humor that will be widely understood. If you have to explain why something is funny, don't include it.

> If you feel uneasy about a joke or an image, don't use it.

> Don't shoehorn humor into your presentation. Include humor when it fits naturally, and is an integral part of the presentation.

> Resist acting like a stand-up comedian. (Unless, of course, you are a stand-up comedian.)

> Avoid sarcasm or humor that targets entire groups, such as racist or sexist jokes.

> Take your topic seriously, but don't take yourself so seriously. If you're too serious, it will make you seem unapproachable and defensive. People will sense that if they challenge your message, they'll be challenging you personally.

> ___ EXAMPLES OF STYLE ADJUSTMENTS

Olivia has a highly interactive, engaging style. She is going to give a presentation to a group of researchers who are known for being reserved, although they are also known for their sense of humor. Olivia realizes that they probably won't want to join in and banter during the presentation, but she would like to solicit some ideas from them. She decides to present her material first and hold a formal question-and-answer session at the end. Instead of interacting with people during the presentation, she will limit herself to two or three rhetorical questions. She will also include some humor in her supporting material.

Henry prefers to stand during a presentation, so he can move around. This helps him shake off nervousness and also helps him convey energy. He is presenting to an audience that prefers presenters to stay seated. They close ranks against people who break the pattern. They don't like people to set themselves apart in any way. So Henry has decided to build in a reason for standing: he's going to use a flip chart or a whiteboard for a presentation aid. This will give him a reason to stand and move around without seeming to defy his audience just for the sake of defying them.

> Style is not something
you acquire; it's some-
thing you have.

> Give yourself permis-
sion to show your
natural style.

> Stylistic features
make your presen-
tations memorable.

> Effective presenters
have a repertoire of
stylistic techniques
they can draw on to
fit the situation and
the audience.

> Adjust to the situa-
tion, the topic, and
the tone.

> Make subtle adjust-
ments in your style,
not large-scale
overhauls.

Martin learned a tough lesson. He was known for his ironic
sense of humor, but as he rose through the ranks, he didn't
realize that people didn't always appreciate or understand his
humor. One day he referred to a serious situation as "the absurd
predicament." People misunderstood him, and he spent the
next week explaining why he had trivialized a potential crisis.
He found out that his humor was often perceived as ridicule
or sarcasm, which was far from what he intended. Martin
began to pay more attention to how he used humor, and he
shifted to self-deprecating humor.

CHAPTER 9 ___ STRATEGY

If you want to take your presentations to the next level, you need to approach them strategically. A strategic approach differs from a basic approach in two ways. First, it emphasizes the role of the audience to a greater extent. Second, it requires a certain skill and experience level as a presenter, so that you can identify your options and effectively adapt your approach.

As a presenter, you can choose to be strategic in every presentation you give, although not every situation requires a strategic approach. It depends on your purpose, the situation, and your audience.

Examples of when a strategic approach is necessary:

> You want to build goodwill with a new team.

> You want to persuade people to take action.

> You face a skeptical, resistant audience.

> You're asking people to make a significant change.

> You want a group to realign their priorities.

> Your biggest client is threatening to walk.

> You're seeking approval and funding from senior management or the company board.

> You need to talk to the press during an organizational crisis.

> ___ MAKING A PRESENTATION STRATEGIC

Preparation for a strategic presentation is more intense than for a regular presentation. You approach the presentation with greater awareness, more intention, and an emphasis on what it takes to achieve a precise objective with an audience. When you're strategic, you're not trying to hit a target; you're aiming for the bull's-eye.

A strategic approach requires a wide range of skills. You have to understand both the broad context and the nuances of details. You prepare extensively and react on the spot. You combine presentation elements while you're fine-tuning individual elements. Some of the skills and tools include:

> careful and vigorous thinking, questioning, analyzing, and calculating

> a clear and explicit purpose

> a detailed plan to reach your objective

> a keen sense of timing

> confidence to fine-tune your approach

> courage to seize opportunities

We have covered many of these topics in previous chapters, including the purpose and confidence. Here are some additional tips to help you apply a strategic perspective.

Analysis and Preparation

When you plan a strategic presentation, don't start with what you would like to say. Start with what the audience wants, needs, and expects to hear. As you do your NASA (Needs/Audience/Situation Analysis), look at each area from the perspective of the audience. For example:

> What is the audience's situation? What events or developments led up to this situation?

> What is the audience concerned about?

> What are their opinions about the issue?

> What are their agendas regarding the issue?

> What are their "hot buttons," or important concerns you should definitely address or absolutely avoid?

> What are the similarities and differences between viewpoints in the audience?

> What are the differences between your views and theirs?

> Are there areas of common ground you could leverage in some way?

> What is happening in other areas of the business?

Timing

Timing is vital when it comes to strategy. You need to consider when you should introduce a topic, give details, or pause for an overview. Consider the following questions as you prepare your presentation:

> What is the most opportune time to present the information?

> How many times have they heard the same message?

> Has enough time passed so that they're ready to hear the message again?

> What was their reaction in the past?

> Do you think they will have a different reaction this time? Why? How can you make sure?

> Has something transpired to make them more receptive to your message this time?

> Do you need to deliver the message now? Is this your window of opportunity?

Courage and Confidence

Presenters need courage and confidence to seize opportunities. You might not have another chance to deliver your message in such a personalized way to this audience. As you prepare your presentation, you have to decide whether you have the courage to:

> Do what you think will work, not just play it safe.

> Be as direct as you need to be.

> Use precise language and not dilute your message.

> Deliver tough or uncomfortable messages.

You also need to assess whether you have the confidence to:

> Believe that your message is worth communicating.

> Assess the situation correctly and make the best choices.

> Connect with the audience.

> Read the audience and make adjustments as you present.

To develop courage and confidence, you have to put yourself into situations where they are needed. For many presenters, this is not a problem—simply getting up in front of a group takes courage and confidence! In this case, however, we're not talking about stage fright; we're talking about following through on your plan. You made it to the threshold, now you need to walk in.

Thorough preparation will bolster your courage and confidence. If you know that you understand the issues and chose the best course, then you will be more likely to follow through. As an added boost, think of the consequences of *not* following through. What will happen if you back down and fail to deliver your message?

> ___ FINE-TUNING YOUR PRESENTATION

Strategic presentations need to be carefully crafted. As you finalize your presentation, do the following:

> Talk to at least two trusted colleagues who have experience with the issue and the audience. Discuss your message and approach. Rely on their insights and modify your presentation as necessary.

> Practice your entire presentation several times. This is an ideal time to videotape your practice sessions and go over them in minute detail. Look at both how you present each element and how the presentation hangs together as a whole.

> ___ PRACTICING PRESENTATION SKILLS

Developing presentation skills is like learning to play tennis. You can quickly learn the basics of the game and have a good time playing occasionally. But if you want to get better, you need to immerse yourself in the game. Watch better players and learn from them. Practice and experiment with new approaches. As you improve, reflect on what works and what doesn't. Gradually, your work will pay off. Conscious decisions will become second-nature responses.

Comparison between improving tennis skills and improving presentation skills

Tennis	Presentations
read your opponent	understand the audience
anticipate where the ball is going	anticipate what the audience wants to know
improve the speed and placement of your serve	improve your introduction
improve your mental game—stay in the match until the end	keep your concentration throughout the presentation
control the point, not just react	control the situation, not just react
move better on the court	use appropriate movement and gestures
mix up your shots	include a mix of supporting material
learn when to come to the net	know how to emphasize key messages
change your game when it's not working	make adjustments during the presentation
fix mistakes	recover gracefully when you make a mistake
use the whole court; place the ball where you want it	be familiar with strategic and stylistic tools and techniques, and be able to use them at will

> ___ LEARNING FROM EXAMPLES

Hearing about other presenters' experiences can be useful in looking for new ideas or things to watch out for. Here are several stories, each one focusing on a single strategic issue.

Bottom Line

Leanne is leading the charge for knowledge management at her organization. The first year, it was no problem getting funding and personnel. The company was doing well, the stock was valued high, and capturing information was a hot topic. Two years later, it's a different story. Her organization is facing intense financial problems, and a knowledge-management initiative seems like a luxury. Suddenly, support for her work has evaporated.

Leanne plans to deliver a status report to her boss and make the case for continuing her work. She has several goals:

> She will convey confidence in the value of her work. She wants to avoid nonverbal features that might make her seem dejected, pessimistic, or defeated. She will speak with a strong voice, use a lot of eye contact, and smile. She will lean forward in her chair and use gestures to show energy and enthusiasm.

> She knows that financial concerns are uppermost in her boss's mind so she will address the financials early in her presentation. She will prepare a cost/benefit analysis and take along statistics, charts, and graphs in a handout.

> She has three success stories of how her work has already paid off. She will highlight her work's short-term positive impact so she can buy more time to complete her long-range plans.

Building a Reputation as a Business Leader

Anne, a senior vice president and chief technology officer, is scheduled to present to the company's board, which includes senior executives. In the past, Anne's presentations have fallen a bit flat. People believe that she can see issues only from the perspective of an engineer, not a business leader. Anne wants and needs to change that perception.

One thing Anne has learned is that she consistently covers *who, what, where, when,* and *how,* but often fails to cover *why*. She makes recommendations but doesn't tie them to a business rationale. People are left to answer the "so what?" question on their own. In this presentation she is going to do two things. First, she will explicitly state the business rationale up front, before she delves into details. Second, she will tie her recommendations to business priorities and initiatives already under way in the company. This will foster the perception that she understands how the business works, where it is now, and how her recommendations will affect groups across the organization.

Courage in the Lion's Den

Sarah has been asked to give a marketing presentation to a senior management group at her organization. This is the first time she has been selected, and she wants to make a good impression. Unfortunately, her topic is not going to make her audience feel warm and fuzzy. She believes the organization has made erroneous assumptions about its customers and the marketplace, and she has several recommendations for changing course.

Sarah knows that her credibility is on the line. According to her sources, the audience will give her a chance to make her case, but it better be solid. They don't have any patience for vague pronouncements. During her practice sessions, Sarah works hard at articulating each key message in a calm, confident manner. She uses a strong voice and eliminates qualifying words.

Sarah will acknowledge their common goals during her background remarks. She wants to establish that she and the audience are on the same side. As she moves through her key messages, she will use vivid examples of companies that stumbled because of their assumptions about their markets and customers. As she makes her recommendations, she will clarify how her proposals will affect both the top and the bottom line.

Internal Partner, Not a Paper Pusher

Steve, a human resources manager, is introducing a new competency model and related performance management tools in his organization. He knows these tools will sound like a lot of paper work to many managers, and they will not recognize how helpful the tools could be. Therefore, he will begin by talking about the organization's goals, and how people's performance directly affects the attainment of those goals. He wants to show that these tools can help the organization achieve its goals, not just make HR look good.

Steve designs his presentation so that every key message emphasizes the partnership between HR and the organization. He will confirm that HR worked with people in the field to create useful tools and demonstrate how the new tools are connected to existing tools, so they won't require a huge learning curve. He will also emphasize how the new tools and processes will make performance management activities more efficient, not more time consuming.

No Backing Down

Scott, a public relations consultant, has been hired by a legal firm to help its staff change their communication style. Their abrasive style not only alienates potential clients but also has been the cause of negative press. But Scott discovers that people at the firm are proud of their tough reputation and have no desire to change. They think it makes them more effective as litigators. Because of this, they are in no mood to listen to an outside flack who probably knows nothing about their work.

Scott decides that this audience is not going to respond well to a kind and gentle manner. Instead, he uses an in-your-face approach. He speaks quickly and forcefully. He makes definitive statements. He doesn't mince words. He looks directly at individuals and asks pointed questions. He doesn't back down from any challenges, and he has an answer for every question.

After 10 minutes, he can tell that they're starting to think he knows what he's talking about. After 20 minutes, he can see people starting to nod their heads and unfold their arms. After 30 minutes, he's got them. Later he hears that it was the first time they thought a PR person understood their work.

Doing the Unexpected

Russell is one of 10 presenters during a two-day conference. He has attended this conference for the past three years and is familiar with the routine. Each presenter shows slides, hands out paper copies of the slides, and spends most of the time clicking through slides. When he last attended, he couldn't remember the difference between the presentations. One year, someone used props instead of slides and it was a breath of fresh air. Russell wants to be the memorable person this year.

He's not going to use any slides. He believes the break in the routine will be memorable and get people out of autopilot so they will pay more attention to his message. He realizes some people will be uncomfortable if they don't have anything to take home, so he'll bring along handouts.

Making Every Minute Count

Carson is feeling the pressure. She has to educate a group quickly on a new project and then convince them to support her with funding. She has only one hour. Two people out of four know a little about the project; the other two are clueless. They are going to be attending meetings all day, and this will be their second to last meeting of the day.

Carson knows she needs to educate people before trying to convince them. They are a savvy, skeptical bunch. She needs to build her rationale, not just announce her findings. She is going to use an inductive structure for her material, building a case for her key messages through examples and statistics. As she moves through her material, she won't belabor obvious points. She plans to briefly acknowledge and affirm what people know, then move on to new information or insights.

Motivating a Team

Victor wants to get his team excited about what they can accomplish in the next year. He knows that genuine enthusiasm shapes people's attitudes more than information does, so he is going to show his attitude through energy, facial animation, vocal expression, and gestures. Victor is also choosing content that appeals to people's emotions. For example:

> He plans to tell several stories that illustrate the kind of effort, attitude, customer service, and other behaviors he wants them to demonstrate.

> He will use language that conveys emotional content. For example, he plans to tell them how proud he is of what the team has done so far and to single out individual accomplishments.

> He is going to use two inspirational quotes.

Appealing to the Senses

George decided to use language that would appeal to key decision makers in his audience. In the weeks before his presentation, he listened carefully to the words they used to determine whether they tended to use visual, audio, or kinesthetic terms. Then he sprinkled those words into his presentation. He made lists for each.

Visual:	see, look, viewpoint, clear, fuzzy, murky, focused, patterns, illuminate
Auditory:	telling, ringing, hearing, humming, resounding, clamoring, discordant, harmonious
Kinesthetic:	dancing along, smooth sailing, gut feeling, bumpy, rocky, balanced, shaky, wrinkled, wrung out, on an even keel

> View your presentation as a high-impact communication opportunity.

> Develop your versatility as a presenter so that you have more strategic options.

> Be clear about what you want to accomplish.

> Design your presentation to meet the expectations of your audience.

> Base strategic decisions on the audience's views about your topic.

> Coordinate clusters of presentation elements to support your strategy.

> Talk *with* people rather than *at* them.

> Recognize that during your presentation you are always selling something: an idea, a proposal or recommendation, the quality of your information or analysis, a product or service, yourself.

Staying on Message

Gwen is a congressional aide who frequently speaks with the press. Her goal is to stay on message, regardless of how reporters try to twist her words or rephrase questions. Her boss is known as a down-to-earth, practical person, and she needs to mirror his behavior and language. She and her colleagues carefully choose the words Gwen will use. They determine when their language needs to match that of other representatives from their party, and when they need to appear independent. They often use inclusive language, with pronouns like "we" and "our." This creates a bond with their constituents. She is careful to avoid off-the-cuff remarks that could come back to haunt her.

Tips for Organizational Cultures

When you give presentations in your organization, take account of your organization's culture, values, and expectations. For example:

> When you present in a sales-oriented culture, make it clear what you are selling: an idea, a proposal, a product. If you are not specific, you will be less likely to get a favorable response. State your objective early in the presentation, either as an attention getter or during the background remarks. Choose supporting material that emphasizes the benefit to the audience.

> When you present in an engineering culture, make your key messages especially clear and concise. Then use precise, detailed supporting material, such as explanations and statistics. For variety, mix in some examples and comparisons.

> When you present in an innovative culture, show your creative side. Highlight new or unique features of your proposal. Play up a unique angle. Show that you have stretched the boundaries in some way.

CHAPTER 10 —— ASK THE COACH

Do you ever wish you could talk to an expert about your presentation? Here are some frequently asked questions and our responses. Our suggestions are based on David Lee's extensive experience as a presenter, the experiences of thousands of people we have coached and trained, and research findings.

As you read them, remember that there is often more than one effective response to a situation. You may think of something we didn't include here. Please send us a letter or an e-mail—we would love to hear your comments, ideas, suggestions, and insights.

> —— PRACTICE AND LEARNING

How do I learn new presentation techniques?

Do what art students do: copy the masters. Analyze each part of their presentations. For example:

> What did they say during the introduction?

> What words did they use for transitions?

> If they told stories, when did they tell them?

> How many questions did they ask?

> What type of humor did they use?

> How did they conclude the presentation?

> What gestures did they use, and how did the gestures support the message?

Always be on the lookout for new concepts, models, principles, and tools. Incorporate them into your "mental model" of presentations and practice them. Mindful practice and specific feedback will help you improve significantly.

I do well during practice, but I freeze when I get in front of an audience.

Learning how to present effectively is like learning any other skill. You can't improve solely by watching other people. You need to get out there, make mistakes and learn how to compensate for them, and learn what works in different situations with different audiences.

Speak more frequently in front of people and build your confidence one step at a time. Start giving short (three to five minutes) presentations in a low-key setting—giving a report at a team meeting, for example. Choose a setting where you can sit down and you don't need presentation aids. Then move on to leading a meeting, where you can practice setting up topics but don't have to speak the entire time. This will give you practice in using presentation aids like flip charts or whiteboards.

How can I get people to give me honest feedback?

Before you ask for feedback, think about how you respond to it. People are not going to be honest with you if you get angry, defensive, or withdrawn. It's OK if you don't agree with them, but guard against being reflexively defensive.

When you ask for feedback, tell people you are eager to improve the effectiveness of your presentations. Then be as specific as you can when you ask for suggestions. If you want comments about delivery, ask about your eye contact, vocal expression, gestures, and so on.

I get conflicting advice about how to give presentations. I just want to know which behaviors are right and which are wrong.

Instead of thinking in terms of right and wrong, think of a spectrum of behavior, from highly effective to highly ineffective. Ask, "What will be the most effective with this audience in this situation?" This will help you determine when you can bend a general guideline.

I feel like I'm never going to get better at giving presentations.

If you decide that you want to improve your speaking skills, you will. We have worked with many people who have improved their effectiveness as presenters, often dramatically.

As you develop your presentation skills, watch out for the trap of trying to do too many new things at one time. You might be excited about improving and jump into it with great enthusiasm only to feel discouraged when you don't see immediate results.

Learning how to give presentations is a step-by-step process. Steady progress, although it is not dramatic at the time, will seem significant when you look back in a few months.

I think it's a waste of time to prepare. I'd rather just wing it.

You may think you can talk your way out of (or through) any situation. But inevitably, the day will come when a lack of preparation won't be charming anymore. Set a minimum standard for the amount of preparation you will do for any presentation—a minimum of more than zero minutes!

Brent Filson, in his book *Executive Speeches* (Wiley, 1994), quotes William C. Ferguson, a former CEO of NYNEX Corporation. "Never give the impression that you haven't prepared. Why should I sit there and listen to somebody who didn't think enough of the audience to prepare?"

I'm too nervous to eat. Will this affect my presentation?

It could. You might feel light-headed or shaky. Don't skip any meals; maintain your usual eating schedule. Depending on the time that you're presenting, you may also want to eat something light an hour or so before you present.

Avoid heavy foods and foods that you know will cause you discomfort. Also avoid milk and citrus drinks; both can give you a dry mouth.

I am part of a group that needs to give a presentation. Do you have any tips for us?

Group presentations fall into one of two categories.

1. Several people participate in one presentation.

2. Several people do separate presentations, based on the same topic or related topics.

When several people are delivering one presentation, consider these tips:

> Have the same person give the introduction and conclusion, or at least the opening and closing remarks. This will provide continuity.

> Decide where mid-presentation hand-offs should occur. The easiest transition points are after the introduction and before the core content, between key messages, or before the conclusion.

> Work out careful transitions. The person finishing one section and the person beginning the next section need to prepare their transitions in advance. Otherwise the hand-off may seem awkward, and the presentation will lose momentum.

If you're doing a series of presentations on a similar topic, consider these tips:

> Think of the presentations as a whole, as an entity that needs an introduction and a conclusion. For continuity purposes, have the same person open and close the program by using basic features of the introduction and conclusion.

> If presenters have similar key messages, have the first presenter give more details about the issue than later speakers.

> Consider having each presenter use the same unifying theme or device—but be aware that overusing a stylistic device can be distracting or can seem like a gimmick.

> ___ THE AUDIENCE

How can I connect with the audience so that I feel like they're for me, not against me?

If you're nervous, you may feel like the audience is a foe. After all, if it weren't for the audience, you wouldn't have to create a presentation!

To connect with an audience, try these things:

> Remember that in most settings, people will be supportive. They know what it's like to give presentations, and they want you to do well. Try not to create adversaries where none exist.

> If you're speaking to a group in which you don't know anyone, make an effort to meet a few people before the presentation. Then you will have some friendly faces to look for.

> If you can't meet anyone beforehand, look over the audience and find people who resemble friends of yours—or pretend certain people are friends—and talk to them.

> Establish points of commonality. During the introduction, show that you share a goal, an experience, a business priority, a value.

> Involve your audience. Ask questions, or invite the audience to share their thoughts on the topic.

> Incorporate humor in an appropriate way. This will show that you take the issue seriously but are able to maintain a sense of humor.

How do I capture people's attention?

When you begin your presentation, show that you are in control. Let the audience wait expectantly for just a moment. This will focus their attention before you start talking. Speak with confidence, purpose, and momentum. Use a strong attention getter in your introduction.

How can I keep people from drifting off during my presentation?

Several factors can cause people's minds to wander. The audience may have been sitting for a long time. They may be thinking about what the last presenter said. They may be thinking about what they have to do when they get back to work. They may be wondering what to have for dinner. In other words, you're just one of many things competing for their attention.

Here are several things you can try:

> As you plan your presentation, think about how you can sequence material and use nonverbals to keep the interest level up. Remember that audiences have more tolerance for content in the morning, so make afternoon speeches livelier.

> Watch more experienced colleagues handle situations in which the audience's attention starts to wander. Note what they do with nonverbals: vary vocal pitch, volume, or pace; use humor; make eye contact with people in the audience. Also observe how they use content to get people back on track. They might tell an anecdote, refer

to members of the audience, or ask a rhetorical question.

> Pair up with a colleague and role-play situations in which the audience gets lost, restless, or otherwise disengaged. Give each other specific feedback on what works well and what is ineffective.

> Ask the group a question, preferably about their experiences. Invite two or three people to share their experiences and observations.

Finally, remember that there are no guarantees. Individuals might be preoccupied by a serious, even tragic, event or problem, and there may be nothing you can do to pull them into your presentation. If that seems to be the case, focus on other listeners.

I think it's important to be responsive to the audience, but I get distracted when people ask questions during the presentation.

Questions can be disruptive, which is why people wait until the end of a presentation to answer them.

One way to handle this is to announce at the beginning of the presentation that you will answer questions at the end, and ask people to hold their questions until then. Of course, that's not always possible or practical, so you need to learn how to deal with interruptions. Practice giving a presentation and ask a colleague to repeatedly interrupt you with questions. This will help you get used to dealing with interruptions without getting rattled.

Memorize or write down a few transition statements you can use to get back to the topic after answering a question. One of the best formats to use consists of a summary plus a forecast. For example, "Not only do we need to be more receptive and responsive to our customer's needs, we also need to anticipate what they will need in the next year, which is the point Terry was raising with his question."

I have to present to an audience that not only disagrees with my ideas but also probably will be unfriendly or hostile toward me personally. What should I do?

This situation requires a strategic approach.

> Explore in depth why people feel this way toward you and your topic.

> Before the presentation, talk to people who will be in the audience so you can hear their points of view on the topic.

> Anticipate confrontational questions and comments and prepare strong, relevant answers.

> Discuss the presentation with a colleague who has presented to this group in the past. Learn about his or her experience and solicit tips on how to proceed.

> Have confidence in what you're going to say.

> Don't overcompensate by being jocular. Humor is a high-risk element in this situation.

> Identify some value or priority that you know you share with the audience and talk about it during your introduction. Emphasizing common ground or a common goal will help you defuse the situation.

> Show that the presentation is a collaborative discussion rather than a competitive debate. When the "adversary" asks a question (even if it sounds like an accusation), turn the question to the group and ask for their thoughts on the issue.

> Do everything you can to treat others in a respectful manner, whether they deserve it or not. You will gain support and respect if you focus on the substantive issue and avoid getting caught up in an adversarial exchange.

I can always count on one of my colleagues to ask an irrelevant question, which frustrates me. How can I answer the question without becoming angry or rude?

First, expect that someone will ask you an irrelevant, tangential, marginally related question. In fact, brainstorm as many of these questions as you can. Then practice how you will answer them calmly, and how you will pull the audience back to an area that is relevant to your message.

As a general guideline, answer a seemingly irrelevant question as concisely as possible. And always be respectful. It may turn out that someone has a good reason to ask an "irrelevant" question.

I'm speaking to an audience whose primary language is different from mine. What should I do?

You can do several things to make yourself easier to understand and to show respect for the audience.

> If you are in another country, greet the audience in the local language. Refer to events and locations from the country or region.

> Speak slower, but not so slowly that you seem condescending.

> Use plain language and terminology.

> Encourage people to ask clarifying questions.

> Explain terminology and acronyms as you go.

> Use examples from everyday life and work experiences.

> If it's appropriate, ask an interpreter to be available.

> ___ MATERIAL

I'm not sure how to pick the correct structure for my presentation.

Sometimes content seems destined for a particular structure; other times it takes trial and error to find an appropriate fit. When you aren't sure, try putting your content into two or three structures that you think might work. Test them out on a friend and discuss which one made the most sense.

> Does the structure allow you to say what you want to say about your subject?

> Will the structure draw the audience in so they become involved in your ideas?

> Will the audience understand the structure?

I've been told that it's hard to understand my presentations because they're disorganized. What can I do?

The most important thing you can do is to use the basic presentation format recommended in this book. These features will help you organize your thoughts, and that organization will be apparent to your listeners. To recap:

1. Introduction (attention getter, background, overview of key messages).

2. Core content (key messages with supporting materials).

3. Conclusion (summary, final emphasis, implication statement).

Ask an experienced presenter to go through your material with you to pinpoint why your presentations seem disorganized. Work together to find effective remedies.

A number of issues may give people the impression you're disorganized. Determine whether these issues are causing you to stumble.

> There is no discernable structure for the content.

> Your structure doesn't fit your content.

> You're not using clear transition statements.

> One of your key messages is actually the purpose of your presentation.

> You put similar information in each key message.

> You go on tangents.

> You frequently make qualifying statements *(it's simple, well, actually it's a little more complicated than that if you factor in all the steps, but basically it's really quite simple if you just stick to the main idea of what it is . . .")*.

Is it OK to use presentation aids during the introduction and conclusion?

The introduction establishes the pattern for the entire presentation. Ideally, it sets a pattern in which the audience pays attention to you, shows interest in the topic, and is favorably inclined toward your purpose. The best way to do this is to establish eye contact between you and the audience. If you start off with a visual, the eye contact will be between the presentation aid and the audience.

If you choose to use a presentation aid during your introduction, use it as an attention getter (but resist creating a slide that says "introduction"—you shouldn't need to reinforce that point). Then stop using visuals when you move to the background remarks. This will give you an opportunity to establish a connection with your listeners.

Similarly, reestablish eye contact with your listeners during your conclusion, especially if you have used several aids during the presentation. Many people use their final presentation aid to review their key messages, then stop using aids when they deliver the final emphasis and the implication statements.

Why do people seem more interested in my secondary points than in my key messages?

Your nonverbal actions may be telling people that your secondary points are more compelling. For example, you might be animated when you tell an anecdote but lose energy when you get back to a key message. Make sure you're equally animated when you deliver your key messages.

How can I alter a standard script to make it seem less canned?

Using a standard script can seem confining, especially if your usual style is informal. If you want to make changes, first find out if changes are allowed. Closely following a script is sometimes necessary—for example, when you deliver a formal statement to the press, or talk to stock analysts about your company.

If changes are allowed, start slowly. Don't try to rebuild the entire presentation. Review the supporting material and determine where you could add or substitute supporting material (especially examples, quotations, or comparisons) to tailor the speech to your style, experience, and audience.

> ___ DELIVERY

I want to come across as an authority on my topic.

Remember, people assess your attitude through your non-verbal behavior. If you act like an authority, they will perceive you as an authority (provided you can back up the perception with content). As you plan and practice your presentation, watch for the following nonverbal and content elements. All of them dilute the perception of authority.

> Your voice goes up at the end of sentences, making you sound like you're questioning yourself.

> You are too soft-spoken; people can't hear you.

> You step back when you deliver key messages.

> You use halfhearted gestures.

> You avoid looking at the audience.

> You frequently break into nervous laughter.

> You use qualifiers and discounting words or phrases *(maybe, sort of, I'd like to, I'm trying to, perhaps)*

> You literally question yourself. *(Is this right? I'm not sure I'm saying this correctly.)*

I'm so scared that I can't look up during the presentation.

Many people feel the same way. Here are some tips:

> Write the words "look at the audience" and "pause and look" in your presentation notes.

> Guard against an all-or-nothing attitude regarding eye contact.

> Practice the following sections of the presentation so that you feel confident enough to look up as you deliver them: the attention getter, at least two places in your core content, and your final emphasis and implication statement.

> Find two or more friendly faces in the audience and look mostly at or toward them. Gradually expand the area where you're looking.

> Practice in front of a couple of colleagues. Make an effort to look at them as often as you can. Have them keep track of how often you looked up, and at what points in the presentation.

How do you get rid of ums and ahs?

Repetitious phrases and vocalized pauses can be distracting. Here is an effective way to reduce the number of times you use them. Ask a friend to listen to you practice your presentation. Every time you use a repetitious phrase, have the person raise his or her hand. After two or three practices with real-time feedback, you will substantially reduce the extent to which you use these phrases.

Focus on minimizing them, not eliminating them entirely. An occasional vocalized pause will go unnoticed.

People tell me I don't show a lot of energy. What can I do?

First, remember that the issue isn't how much energy you feel like showing or want to show, it's how much energy you *need* to show to convey your message effectively.

Next, get feedback from people who have seen you present so you don't have to rely only on your own perceptions. You might think you're being energetic, but it might seem to other people that you are presenting from behind frosted glass: they can barely hear you, they can see some movement and gestures, but all subtlety is lost.

View your presentation as an "enlarged conversation." Think about what you do during an animated conversation with a family member, friend, or colleague. Then try to retain, and enlarge, those features when you give a presentation. Speak with more volume and projection, use larger hand and arm gestures, and use gestures more frequently.

I frequently get the same feedback—slow down.

Several factors may be the culprit. For example:

> You have a monotonous pace. Slow down from time to time, and add pauses to make transitions and emphasize points.

> You show a lot of energy and momentum, but it's too relentless. Shift gears. Speak faster when you present straightforward information, but slow down when you want to give people time to reflect on your words.

> You don't enunciate clearly. Lazy articulation can make you sound like you are speaking too quickly. Enunciate words and phrases more carefully; this will make you slow down.

> You use too many explanations. Because explanations are abstract, listeners need more time to absorb and understand what you're saying. Add other types of supporting materials, especially concrete examples.

Several people have told me to be more concise. What can I do?

Many factors contribute to the impression that you're wordy or long-winded, including:

> unclear purpose and/or key messages

> inappropriate structure

> complicated key messages

> long words in long sentences

> too much supporting material

> too much background information in key messages

> frequent tangents

> too many vague explanations and too few concrete examples

What can you do?

> Once you determine the source of the problem, focus on fixing it. For example, if you find that your key messages are unclear, restate them more precisely, concisely, and crisply.

> List all the supporting material, then rank it according to "must know" and "nice to know."

> Keep track of the type of material you cut. Make sure you keep an appropriate mix of supporting material.

> Determine whether some material could be put in a handout that people could read after the presentation.

> Consider shortening material instead of cutting it. Remember that speaking is different from

writing: it requires shorter sentences, a simpler structure, and few multisyllabic words. Keep it short and simple.

People tell me I'm *too* concise.

Presenters who hear this often feel frustrated. They were told that being concise is a virtue, and now they're being told to add more material. If this happens to you, consider these questions:

> Do you have at least three key messages?

> Do you have at least three pieces of supporting material for each key message?

> Do you use a mix of concrete examples, comparisons, and explanations?

> Do you include background in the introduction?

> Do you make your purpose clear during the introduction?

> Do you use presentation aids? If not, where could you add them?

People tell me not to use so much jargon, but I don't even hear it when I use it.

Jargon pops up in many presentations. Unfortunately, it can become a distraction to some audiences. To check your use of jargon, try the following suggestions:

> First, ask some clarifying questions to learn more about how you use jargon. Are you using it incorrectly? Too frequently? Does it muddle your message?

> Raise your awareness of the jargon used in your industry and at your organization. Start

compiling a list of terms you hear and see. Also get a list from an editor at your organization.

> When you write your presentation notes, circle all jargon words. Determine whether each instance is appropriate or just a buzzword. Keep appropriate terminology, since it will show that you understand the topic and the language your audience uses.

> The first time you use an acronym, explain it. Tell the audience whether you will be using an abbreviated form during the rest of the presentation.

> Ask a colleague to keep track of technical or industry jargon (including acronyms) you used during your presentation. Find out whether it made sense and if it was used correctly.

What's wrong with reading a presentation?

When you write, you expect people to read your words, not listen to them. You have more leeway for long sentences, complicated phrases, and words with many syllables. Whether someone can read an entire sentence in a single breath never crosses your mind. If you write out your entire presentation, you're going to think like a writer, not a speaker. You're going to create sentences that make sense on paper.

What you need to do is to write sentences that make sense when they're spoken. The audience doesn't expect you to speak in perfectly formed paragraphs. In fact, it will seem odd if you do. Write prompts and notes instead of the entire text. This will guarantee that you speak in a way that is meant to be heard, not read.

I get hoarse when I give several presentations within a short period of time. What causes this, and what can I do?

Three things often make people hoarse: they constrict their throat when they speak, they're trying to increase their volume, or their habitual pitch is higher than their optimum pitch. All three are relatively easy to fix.

Relaxing your throat and breathing from your diaphragm will help with constriction and volume. Adjusting your pitch takes a little more practice. Most people have about a two-octave range but use only one octave. Find your range by going to your lowest pitch, then singing do-re-mi until you reach the top. Now find your optimum pitch by counting one-fourth of the way from the bottom of your pitch range. This is probably one or two tones below your habitual pitch. If you use this pitch, it will be more comfortable, you will sound better to the audience, and you will be less hoarse.

Recently a colleague gave a presentation in which he swore and made inappropriate comments. What are the guidelines for this?

In general, avoid words, terms, or expressions that may offend or alienate listeners. Even if people aren't particularly offended, inappropriate language will diminish your credibility.

Use professional language. Do not use obscene language or make racial, ethnic, or sexist references. Depending on the audience, you may even want to avoid slang.

> ___ ADAPTABILITY

How can I improve my ability to think on my feet?

Thinking on your feet is a paradox. You have to be prepared, yet let go and live in the moment. Think of baseball players up to bat. They have spent years at batting practice, learning how to hit different types of pitches. But during the game, they don't have time to analyze pitches and think through their responses. They have to be in the moment and react in a split second to what they're seeing. In other words, they think on their feet. It's the same for presenters. The only way to do this is to know your topic inside and out, then pay attention to the moment.

When you feel stuck during the presentation (the moment of panic), try the following tips:

> Take a moment to pause and collect your thoughts so that when you start talking you won't have to hesitate or hem and haw. Because pauses are used for transitions or emphasis, it may appear to be a natural break.

> If you need a few more seconds, use an appropriate lead-in phrase or question, such as:

   - This issue is complicated; let me think for a moment.

   - Let me share what I know about that issue.

   - What about some of you—what do you know about this issue?

   - Who else is familiar with the initiative we're talking about? What have you heard or seen?

   - Before I go any further, I would like to hear any questions you have about this topic.

Do you have any tips for giving a presentation on the spur of the moment?

Opportunities to give presentations crop up suddenly, especially in a business setting. You should be ready and able to present on any issue or topic that you work with regularly.

Organize your thoughts in the same way you would for any presentation. Start with an attention getter, such as an interesting comment or fact. Then give some background remarks, and highlight two or three aspects of the issue that you want to cover (overview). Address each aspect (your key messages), giving some supporting material. Summarize your key messages, or emphasize one point you want people to remember. Close by stating the next steps, or what you would like people to do (implication statement).

Once you get used to this format, you can use it to quickly organize your thoughts in any situation. You will be able to improvise and still sound prepared.

How can I cut my presentation on the spot? How do I know what to cut and what to keep?

Despite the best-laid plans, sometimes you don't have the time you expected for your presentation. You may be told that your 30-minute presentation just got cut to 10 minutes, or the 2-minute signal comes when you're only on the second of four key messages. Here are some tips:

> Mark sections of your presentation that are essential and sections that are optional.

> Delete the attention getter if it is too long. Write a short statement you could use to replace it.

> Shorten the background/positioning remarks.

> Skip some supporting material.

> Drop one or more key messages.

> Delete the summary of key messages in your conclusion.

What should I do if I can't use my slides?

If the equipment doesn't work or it is incompatible with your computer, you won't be able to use your slides. Instead, try these tips:

> If there is a whiteboard or a flip chart, recreate simple slides.

> Bring along copies of the slides on a handout.

> Resist holding up a printed copy of your slide. The print will be too small, and people will try to read it instead of listen to you.

> ___ GENERAL

If I have a choice, should I sit or stand during the presentation?

When you stand, you make more of an impact. For groups of more than five or six, try to stand. Standing during a presentation puts you in a stronger, more prominent position nonverbally. You can be more active and use gestures, position, and movement to convey interest, enthusiasm, and conviction.

Sometimes people expect you to present from a seated position. If you do, make an effort to establish eye contact. Keep your hands above the table so people can see your gestures. Also, sit on the front part of the chair and lean forward.

During some presentations, you may want to both sit and stand. You might sit during most of the presentation and stand to use a flip chart or whiteboard. Or you could stand to give the presentation but sit down when you take questions. Being at the same eye level as other participants can facilitate a discussion.

What are the advantages and disadvantages of using a lectern?

A lectern provides a place to put your notes and gives you something to hold on to if you're nervous. It also contributes to a sense of formality. On the other hand, a lectern creates both a physical and a psychological distance between you and the audience. It tethers you to one spot and limits your ability to walk around, especially if the microphone is fastened to the lectern.

In general, when you have an option, choose not to use a lectern.

Is it OK to drink water during a presentation?

It depends on the type of presentation. During a long presentation, you may want to have water available. When you moderate a discussion, you have opportunities to take a drink while someone else is talking.

During a short presentation, drinking water may be a distraction to the audience. People could become thirsty when they see you take a drink.

Sometimes the desire to take a drink of water is a nervous gesture, because your throat feels dry. A better option is to coat your throat before speaking by sucking on a small lozenge. Make sure you test the lozenge before you give the presentation. You may find that it is too strong, makes your eyes water, or makes you cough or sneeze. You don't want to start your presentation by snuffling or choking.

What are some tips for using a microphone?

When you use a stationary microphone, keep the microphone between you and the section of audience you are looking at. That way the microphone will be in front of your mouth and pick up the sound of your voice. When you want to be able to move around the presentation area, use a lapel or lavalier microphone that will continue to pick up your voice as you walk around.

Remember that a microphone and sound system cannot take the place of an energetic and expressive voice. A weak, thin monotone will simply be an amplified weak, thin monotone. Strive for effective vocal projection and vocal variety, even if the sound engineer has to turn the volume down.

PRESENTATION TEMPLATE

If you turned to this section, you probably have to give a presentation soon. It's finally gotten to the point where you need to do some planning. This template will help you organize and coordinate your content, nonverbal actions, and presentation aids. It will also help you see the flow of your presentation.

Using this template will help you significantly improve how you prepare and deliver presentations. It will make the preparation process less confusing and haphazard. You will find that your presentations are clearer, and easier for the audience to follow.

As you develop your presentation skills, remember the three P's: persistence, preparation, and practice. Good luck!

> ____ SEQUENCE FOR FILLING OUT THE TEMPLATE

1. State your purpose. Doing this first is both symbolic and practical. It will prod you to clarify why you are giving this presentation, and it will give you a standard you can use to determine whether material is appropriate for the presentation.

2. Determine your core content. (There is room on this template for five messages; use three to five messages for your presentation.) Fill in each key message and its supporting material. Check to see if you have a solid mix and variety of supporting material spread across the key messages. Try to use at least four types in your presentation.

3. Write the introduction.

   a. Find a way to capture the audience's attention. Give them a reason to listen further.

   b. Provide background material that your audience needs in order to understand your key messages. Stay away from tangential content.

   c. Give a short overview of your key messages so the audience knows what to expect.

4. Write the conclusion.

   a. Summarize your key messages to solidify them in the minds of your audience.

   b. Emphasize one point you want people to remember. (If they remember nothing else, they should remember this.)

   c. Write your implication statement. Tell the audience how you want them to respond to your message. Be specific.

5. Choose transition statements that tie your key messages together and facilitate the flow of your presentation.

6. Select presentation aids that illuminate your message. Think about expanding beyond slides and handouts.

7. Choreograph any nonverbals that you need to practice— actions that don't come naturally.

Presentation Template		
Purpose		
Introduction	*Attention getter* **Presentation aid(s)** *Background* *Overview of key messages*	**Nonverbal actions**
Core Content	**Key message #1** **Presentation aid(s)** *Supporting material* *Transition statement*	
	Key message #2 **Presentation aid(s)** *Supporting material* *Transition statement*	
	Key message #3 **Presentation aid(s)** *Supporting material* *Transition statement*	
	Key message #4 **Presentation aid(s)** *Supporting material* *Transition statement*	
	Key message #5 **Presentation aid(s)** *Supporting material* *Transition statement*	
Conclusion	*Summarize key messages* **Presentation aid(s)** *Final emphasis* *Implication statement*	

RECOMMENDED RESOURCES

> ___ INDIVIDUAL COACHING

Individuals can work directly with PDI Ninth House presentation consultants, such as David Lee, to improve their presentation skills.

> ___ BOOKS

D'Aprix, Roger. *Communicating For Change: Connecting the Workplace with the Marketplace.* Hoboken, NJ: Jossey-Bass, 1996. ISBN: 0787901997.

Holliday, Micki. *Secrets of Power Presentations, 2nd edition.* Franklin Lakes, NJ: Career Press, 2000. ISBN: 1564144380.

Jacobi, Jeffrey. *How to Say It with Your Voice.* Paramus, NJ: Prentice Hall Press, 2000. ISBN: 0735201528.

Ringle, William. *Techedge: Using Computers to Present and Persuade.* Boston: Allyn & Bacon, 1997. ISBN: 020527305X.

The Forbes Book of Business Quotations. New York: Black Dog & Leventhal Publishers, Inc., 1997. ISBN: 1884822622.

Urech, Elizabeth. *Speaking Globally: Effective Presentations Across International and Cultural Boundaries, 2nd edition.* London: Kogan Page Ltd., 2002. ISBN: 0971761507.

Woodall, Marian K. *Thinking on Your Feet: How to Communicate Under Pressure.* Bend, OR: Professional Business Communications, 1996. ISBN: 0941159965.

Zarefsky, David. *Public Speaking: Strategies for Success, 3rd edition.* Boston: Allyn & Bacon, 2001. ISBN: 0205334431.

ABOUT THE AUTHORS

> ⎯⎯ DAVID G. LEE

David G. Lee, Executive Consultant at Personnel Decisions International, specializes in communication consulting, management and leadership training, team building, and executive coaching. He has trained over 30,000 people in the presentation principles found in this book.

For more than 25 years, Lee has advised and coached executives and managers from organizations across a wide range of industries, including Bank of America, Donaldson Company, Inc., Deluxe Corporation, Eaton Corporation, Medtronic, Inc., 3M, National Association of Industrial and Office Properties, PepsiCo, Target Corporation, Texas Instruments, Toys "R" Us, Inc., and Wells Fargo.

Lee is a co-author of PDI's *Successful Executive's Handbook* and the *Successful Manager's Handbook*.

> ⎯⎯ KRISTIE J. NELSON-NEUHAUS

Kristie J. Nelson-Neuhaus is Editor-in-Chief of Personnel Decisions International's publishing program. She has edited and co-written several of PDI's titles, including the *Successful Executive's Handbook,* the *Successful Manager's Handbook,* the *Leader as Coach Workbook,* and the *Development FIRST Workbook.* Over the past six years, she has coached dozens of clients through PDI's "Speaking with Impact" program. Nelson-Neuhaus is a graduate of the University of California, Los Angeles.

ABOUT PDI NINTH HOUSE

PDI Ninth House is a premier global leadership solutions company with distinctive expertise in accelerating leadership effectiveness to maximize organizational performance. We have over 40 years of experience in helping clients identify, manage, develop, and promote superior leaders across all levels of client organizations. We serve thousands of clients on six continents, including 70 percent of the BusinessWeek Top 100 Global Brands, 75 percent of the Forbes Global 100 and 80 percent of the FORTUNE 100 firms in the United States.

PDI Ninth House partners with large global organizations to solve a wide range of leadership challenges, using a unique combination of innovative, field-tested strategies, state-of-the-art technology, and proven processes to tailor specific solutions for clients.

We help organizations:

> Identify, place, and maintain leadership talent at all levels

> Assess performance, potential, readiness, and fit for leadership transitions

> Develop and train current and future leaders at all levels from individual contributors to managers, executives, and CEOs

> Coach individuals to improve their leadership effectiveness

> Drive a human capital strategy that aligns talent with business and organizational strategy

> Plan for succession to promote and deploy the right people at the right time

> Provide stellar change management programs that create lasting behavior change in organizations

> Use technology to deliver rapid, cost-effective training to address the learning needs of all demographic groups globally

> Drive behavior change through highly engaging learning experiences that speak to the hearts and minds of today's learners

Leaders make or break organizations at all levels. We look forward to exploring how we can help you.

www.pdininthhouse.com

1.800.633.4410 (North America)
+32.2.7777.020 (Europe)
+65.6732.2252 (Asia)

salesreferral@pdininthhouse.com

A

keeping people from drifting off tips, 112–113
in Needs/Audience/Situation Analysis (NASA), 6–7
audio presentation aids, tips for using, 37

B

background information, providing in introductions, 23
breathing, vocal expression and, 55–56

C

chronological organization, for key messages, 11
classification organization, for key messages, 12
climax organization, for key messages, 12
clothing, confidence building and, 75
color, presentation aids tips for, 34
comparisons, as supporting material, 16
complexity, levels of, for key message organization, 13
conclusions, 25–26
    emphasize one point in, 25–26
    implication statement, 26
    key points to remember, 28
    presentation aids during, 117–118
    recap key messages in, 25
confidence building, 69–80
    adaptability and, 79–80
    clothing and appearance, 75
    day of presentation, 74–76
    dealing with tension, 76
    fear and confidence, 69
    getting flustered, 78
    key points to remember, 80
    losing your place, 78–79
    overview chart for, 71
    preparation and practice, 73–74

expressiveness, 45–56
    attitudes, 46–47
    facial expressions and eye contact, 50–51
    gestures and movement, 47–50
    importance of, 45
    key points to remember, 56
    vocal expression, 51–56
eye contact
    looking at audience tips, 119–120
    nonverbal communication, 50–51

F

facial expression, nonverbal communication, 50–51
feedback
    honest feedback from audience, 108
flip charts, tips for using, 38
formality, presentation style and, 88–89
formal presentations, 88
funnel structure
    for answering questions, 61–62
    for key messages, 13

G

gestures, nonverbal communication, 47–50
group presentations, 110–111

H

hand gestures, nonverbal communication, 49–50
handouts, tips for using, 38–39
hostile audience tips, 114–115
humor
    as introduction, 22
    as supporting material, 20
    tips for using effectively, 92–93

transitions, 24–25
   importance of, 24
   key points to remember, 28
   types of, 24–25

U

unifying device, for key message, 14–15

V

videotaping presentation
   confidence building and, 73–74
   fine-tuning presentation, 99
   identifying your style and, 82–83
visualization, confidence building and, 71–73
visual presentation aids, tips for using, 37
vocal expression, 51–56
   articulation, 52
   breathing and, 55–56
   getting rid of ums/ahs, 120
   hoarseness, 125
   inflection, 52–53
   mispronunciation, 52
   pace, 53–54
   quality, 54–55
   slowing down tips, 121
   verbal style tips, 84–85
   volume and projection, 55–56

W

water during presentation, 129
Web sites, as presentation aid, and tips for using, 44
whiteboards, tips for using, 38